INNOVATIONS IN STRESS
AND HEALTH

INNOVATIONS IN STRESS AND HEALTH

Edited by

Susan Cartwright

Professor of Organizational Psychology and Well Being and Director of the Centre for Organizational Health and Well Being, Lancaster University, UK

and

Cary Cooper

Distinguished Professor of Organizational Psychology and Health, Lancaster University

First published 2011 by
PALGRAVE MACMILLAN

Palgrave Macmillan in the UK is an imprint of Macmillan Publishers Limited,
registered in England, company number 785998, of Houndmills, Basingstoke,
Hampshire RG21 6XS.

Palgrave Macmillan in the US is a division of St Martin's Press LLC,
175 Fifth Avenue, New York, NY 10010.

Palgrave Macmillan is the global academic imprint of the above companies
and has companies and representatives throughout the world.

Palgrave® and Macmillan® are registered trademarks in the United States,
the United Kingdom, Europe and other countries.

ISBN 978–0–230–25191–5

This book is printed on paper suitable for recycling and made from fully
managed and sustained forest sources. Logging, pulping and manufacturing
processes are expected to conform to the environmental regulations of the
country of origin.

A catalogue record for this book is available from the British Library.

A catalog record for this book is available from the Library of Congress.

10   9   8   7   6   5   4   3   2   1
20   19   18   17   16   15   14   13   12   11

Printed and bound in Great Britain by
MPG Group, Bodmin and King's Lynn

CONTENTS

CONTENTS

LIST OF FIGURES

LIST OF CONTRIBUTORS

Hilary Abernethy, BSc (Hons), RGN, RMN, has worked in the field of mental health for over 25 years. She is currently Senior Public Health Improvement Specialist and Equality and Human Rights Lead Officer at North Lancashire Primary Care Trust.

Mark Blundell has worked for McDonald's for over 20 years and is Head of HR Operations, Talent and Resourcing.

Susan Cartwright, BA (Hons), MSc, PhD, is Professor of Organizational Psychology and Well Being and Director of the Centre for Organizational Health and Well Being at Lancaster University. She is a fellow of the British Psychological Society and a fellow of the British Academy of Management and has worked in the area of stress and health for over 20 years.

Cary L. Cooper, CBE, PhD, is Distinguished Professor of Organizational Psychology and Health at Lancaster University Management School, Chair of the Academy of Social Sciences, and President of the British Association of Counselling and Psychotherapy, and was lead scientist in the UK Government Office for Science Foresight project on Mental Capital and Wellbeing.

John Cooper has recently retired as Head of Corporate Occupational Health at Unilever Plc.

Sue C. Connelly MA, Dip Counseling, is Global Health and Wellbeing Director at AstraZeneca. She has worked for

AstraZeneca for over 25 years, where she has developed a counseling and life management program to support mental wellbeing within the organization. She is currently responsible for developing and delivering their Global Health & Wellbeing strategy and vision, alongside Eric Teasdale.

Philip Gibbs recently completed his PhD at Lancaster University and is currently Head of Wellbeing at Roodlane Medical.

Andrew Kinder, MSc, AFBPsS, MAC, MBACP, FBACP Registered Practitioner Psychologist, is a chartered Counseling and Occupational Psychologist. Andrew joined the Post Office in 1995 and was transferred to Royal Mail Group's outsourced OH Provider, Atos Healthcare, in 2002. He is Chief Psychologist.

Richard Park MBACP, CQSW, MA, Diploma in Organizational Counselling is a BACP accredited counselor. He joined the Post Office Welfare department in 1992 and was transferred to Royal Mail Group's outsourced OH provider, Atos Healthcare, in 2002.

Dean Patterson is Global Health and Productivity manager at Unilever Plc.

Eric L. Teasdale MB.ChB, FRCP, FFOM, FRCGP is the Chief Medical Officer – Global Health and Wellbeing for AstraZeneca. Eric is also an Honorary Professor at the School of Health and Medicine, Lancaster University.

Su Wang, MBBS, FFOM, MScom, DIH, DPH, DMS, CAM, SFIIRSM, MIEHF, is an accredited Specialist Occupational Physician and was Group Head of Health in Royal Mail from 2002 to 2009. She is a fellow of the Faculty of Occupational Medicine and a qualified coach. Her work at Royal Mail won several prestigious awards and showed a contribution of £227 million to Royal Mail.

CHAPTER 1

INTRODUCTION

Susan Cartwright and Cary L. Cooper

The costs of stress and ill health to society are enormous. The recent report by Black (2008) commissioned by the UK government on the health of the working age population estimated the annual cost of sickness absence and workless-ness associated with working-age ill health to be in excess of £100 billion. Stress-related conditions, such as anxiety and depression, are the second most common reason for absence from work in the UK (HSE 2006) and Europe, and the World Health Organization (WHO) predicts that by 2020 five of the top ten medical problems worldwide will be stress-related. In addition, stress has been shown to be a predictor of work-related accidents and safety errors (Clarke 2008). In the wider population, one in four people experiences mental ill health problems each year and nearly a third of all diseases and disabilities are linked to people's lifestyle behaviors.

Recent estimates in the UK (Sainsbury Centre for Mental Health 2007) suggest that lost days due to mental ill health problems cost employers £8.4 billion per year. However, it is also estimated that the costs of presenteeism, that is employees attending work when they are not fit to do so, are even higher and amount to a staggering £15.1 billion in terms of reduced productivity.

The Health and Safety Executive (2006) defines stress as 'the adverse reaction people have to excessive pressure or other demands placed on them'. In the work environment, stress arises when the demands of work exceed the

1

employee's ability to cope with or control them. An impor-tant distinction is made between pressure, which can be positive if managed correctly, and stress, which can be detrimental to health. The potential sources of stress at work are many and various and include excessive workload, unclear roles, lack of adequate support and supervision, poor or abusive relationships, organizational change and poor work–life balance.

In recent years, organizations have been increasingly encouraged to regularly assess the physical and psychoso-cial hazards in the workplace that present a risk to employee health and to take steps to eliminate and/or moderate these risks through the conduct of stress or wellbeing audits. As a means of addressing workplace health problems, many organizations provide employee counseling services, stress management and resilience training as well as engaging in health promotion activities such as health screening, lifestyle advice, smoking cessation and exercise programs.

However, it is still the case that the proportion of the general working population with access to occupational health services varies significantly from 43 percent in the health and social services sectors to 1 percent in agriculture, forestry and fishing (McDonald 2002) and that such ser-vices are concentrated among a few large employers. Recent evidence from 55 case studies in the UK has demonstrated a strong business case for investment in employee health (Price Waterhouse Cooper 2008), yet investment in such activities is still typically a low priority compared with other areas of organizational expenditure.

A GREATER FOCUS ON WELLBEING

Several decades of stress research have been extremely influ-ential in emphazising the causal link between excessive stress and ill health and how important it is that employers act to ensure that employees are not made ill or harmed by their work.

However, the absence of stress is not necessarily an indicator of a healthy individual or a healthy organization. As long ago as 1946, the World Health Organization defined health as a 'state of complete physical, mental and social well being and not merely the absence of disease or infirmity'.

Wellbeing is a subjective concept experienced through the presence of pleasant emotions such as self-evaluated happiness, through the engagement in interesting and fulfilling activities and the generalized feelings of satisfaction with life. Interestingly, the correlation between wellbeing and income is relatively low in modern industrialized economies, suggesting that material wealth in itself does not make people happy (Myers 2000).

Indeed, the recent Foresight report published by the UK Government Office for Science (2008) associates health and wellbeing with creative thinking, productivity, good interpersonal relationships and resilience in the face of adversity as well as good physical health and life expectancy. Such ideas are reflected in the upsurge in interest in positive psychology (Seligman 1991), which encourages the study of the conditions and processes that contribute to the flourishing and optimal functioning of people, groups and institutions. Proponents of positive psychology argue that an energized workforce is one which is positively engaged, where employees work well together, relationships are supportive and inspiring and information is freely shared (Cross *et al.* 2003). Given that the experience of stress is the outcome of being overwhelmed by negative emotions, the promotion and development of positive emotions is considered to be a major factor in health improvement.

OVERVIEW OF THIS BOOK

This book brings together the contributions of chief medical officers, human resource directors, leading health professionals and consultants to share their practices and perspectives on recent and emergent innovations in the field of stress and health.

In Chapter 2, Teasdale and Connelly describe the perspective that their company, AstraZeneca, adopts in relation to employee health. AstraZeneca has had in place a long-term multilevel strategy for promoting staff wellbeing since the mid-1980s. In this chapter, the authors outline how this strategy has evolved from a focus primarily on stress management and stress reduction to a more holistic and positive approach in which energy management is regarded as being pivotal to high performance.

The theme of Chapter 3 by Cartwright and colleagues at Unilever is the relationship between health and employee engagement. The chapter reports on the impact that participation in the multi-modular Lamplighter program has had not only in improving the health and wellbeing of employees at Unilever but also its contribution to business outcomes. Cartwright *et al.* also provide a good model by which organizations can collect valuable data by which to demonstrate the business case for investment in health promotion activities.

In Chapter 4, Blundell presents a comprehensive overview of the wellbeing strategy developed by McDonald's. The organization employs a widely diverse workforce in terms of age and social background, yet ably demonstrates how the company was able to develop a holistic wellbeing strategy that successfully creates a fusion between business needs and employee values. Furthermore, the organization shows how technology can become a key enabler in the delivery of wellbeing initiatives.

For many years, Royal Mail Group has been at the leading edge of mental health support in the UK workplace and has received many awards for its work. In Chapter 5, Wang and colleagues review the range of initiatives that form part of the integrated systemic approach which the organization has developed and refined over time, working in partnership. These initiatives range from absence management consultancy, stress management and resilience training to rehabilitation programs.

Finally, in Chapter 6, Abernethy steps outside the workplace and adopts a wider public health perspective in arguing for the value of social prescribing as mechanism for promoting emotional wellbeing. Once again, social prescribing is a holistic approach to health improvement with a strong focus on creating a sense of purpose and enjoyment through engagement in artistic and creative activities, learning new skills, volunteering and befriending as well as more traditional stress management education and techniques.

In compiling this book we are extremely grateful to our contributors for the quality and diversity of the chapters they have produced and hope that their contributions will be an inspiration to those in the field of health and wellbeing. Our thanks also extend to the practical help and support of Gerry Wood at Lancaster University and the editorial team at Palgrave Macmillan.

REFERENCES

Black, C. (2008) *Working for a Healthier Tomorrow* (London: Crown Publications).

Clarke, S. (2008) 'Accidents and safety in the workplace', in S. Cartwright and C. L Cooper (eds), *The Oxford Handbook of Organizational Well Being* (Oxford: Oxford University Press).

Cross, R., Baker, W. and Parker, A. (2003) 'What creates energy in organizations?' *MIT Sloan Management Review*, 44 (4): 51–56.

Foresight (2008) *Mental Capital and Wellbeing: Making the Most of Ourselves in the 21st Century* (London: Crown Publications).

HSE (2006) *Workplace Health and Safety Survey* (London: Health and Safety Executive).

McDonald, J. C. (2002) 'The estimated workforce served by occupational physicians in the UK', *Journal of Occupational Medicine*, 52 (7): 401–406.

Myers, D. G. (2000) 'The funds, friends and faith of happy people', *American Psychologist*, 55 (1): 56–67.

Price Waterhouse Cooper (2008) *Building the Case for Wellness* (London: PWC).

Sainsbury Centre for Mental Health (2007) *Mental Health at Work: Developing the Business Case* (London: Centre for Mental Health).

Seligman, M. (1991) *Learned Optimism* (New York: Free Press).

CHAPTER 2

IS PRESSURE OR ENERGY MANAGEMENT THE KEY TO HIGH PERFORMANCE?

Eric L. Teasdale and Sue C. Connelly

INTRODUCTION

If organizations want high performance from their employees, should they focus on pressure management or energy management?

Traditionally, the focus of stress management has been on the negative elements of the working environment, helping employers to focus on the underlying causes and implementing strategies to aid their prevention either at an individual and/or an organizational level. These strategies are often multidimensional, targeting cognitive ability. The deployment of technology – for example 'Smart' phones such as BlackBerries and iPhones, WiFi capability – and time management training are aimed at assisting individuals to better cope with the demands placed upon them and the resultant 'pressure'.

Organizations need to deliver sustained high performance to remain competitive and productive in their field in the long term. In order to do this a lean, agile, fully motivated workforce is required, where all individuals are energized to reach their full potential, are fully engaged and deliver continuous productivity improvements. A healthy, energized workforce requires a baseline standard to avoid long-term illness and, beyond a median performance level, may present an opportunity for competitive advantage. Key to this is the concept of energy management.

If we want individuals to perform well for many years, those individuals need to understand what is likely to maintain their health and wellbeing and help them thrive. The human mind and body are complex and we need to address all aspects of health and wellbeing.

Sustained high achievement demands physical and emotional strength as well as sharp intellect. To bring mind, body and spirit to peak condition, and keep them there, we need to learn that recovering energy is as important as expending it.

This chapter will describe the advantages of moving the paradigm of pressure management to one of energy management. This approach is being taken in AstraZeneca, where we both work.

Let's start with the fundamentals: let's define *health* in its widest context. *Wellbeing* is a much broader concept, which is also worth exploring.

When 'health' starts to suffer, in the work context, it's often related to so-called *mental health* or, more exactly, ill health. *Stress* is often the result. Stress is not an illness in itself but a powerful cause of illness, and one that will be explored in this chapter. We shall ask what stress is and what organizations and individuals can do about it.

People who are 'healthy' usually have high *energy* levels. Can 'energy' be enhanced and improved? How can this be achieved? These are questions we shall explore in this chapter.

WHAT IS 'HEALTH'?

The World Health Organization (WHO) defines health as 'a state of complete physical, mental and social wellbeing and not merely the absence of disease or infirmity' (WHO 1948). Many of the 'physical' aspects of health in the workplace are now well understood (e.g. dermatitis and asthma related to exposure to allergens at work). However, over the last 10 to 20 years, the mental and social aspects of health have come more into focus and are often difficult to understand and manage.

One group of managers attending a conference was asked to come up with their own definitions for health, without referring to a dictionary. One said, '*Health is having an empty medicine chest, well used trainers and not knowing who your family doctor is.*' It's very easy to 'medicalize' any definition of 'health', but it should, rather, be thought of in a broad sense. Let's consider four categories in order to offer a variety of definitions for 'health', gleaned by one of the authors over the last few decades. The first defines health in *common sense* terms, putting it in perspective; then comes a view of the '*struggle*' to attain health; this is followed by 'health' in terms of enjoyment, pleasure, happiness and quality of life (*the 'positives' of health*).

Common sense definitions

When neither the mind nor the body is in a condition to stop the individual from doing what he or she wishes.

Health is a personal quality that enables a particular individual to utilize his or her full potential in the pursuit of living satisfaction within a given environment.

(Greene 1974).

The nearest approach to health is a physical and mental state fairly free from discomfort and pain, which permits the person concerned to function as effectively and as long as possible in the environment where chance or choice has placed them.

(René Dubos, French microbiologist).

Is achieving health a 'struggle' – perhaps something which cannot be fully achieved?

The concept of perfect and positive health is a utopian creation of the human mind. It cannot become reality because man will never be so perfectly adapted to his environment that his life will not involve struggles, failure and sufferings ... nevertheless, the utopia of positive health constitutes a creative force ... it becomes a dangerous mirage only when its unattainable character is forgotten.

(René Dubos, French microbiologist)

Perhaps 'health' can be defined in positive terms – the following definitions 'talk of' enjoyment, pleasure, quality of life and happiness.

Our aim must be not mere absence of gross diseases or disability but positive health overflowing in joy and vitality. Nothing is good enough except the very highest health of which each individual is intrinsically capable.

(Cyril Bibby, biologist and educator, 1914–1987).

A justified feeling of mental and physical well-being enabling good quality of life.

A state of mind and body which permits happiness – without undue reliance on the healthcare professions.

... a personal experience of positive enjoyment of life
(Dalzell Ward and Pirrie 1962).

As doctors we are in danger of being cast in the bleak role of saying 'no' to so many things; eating, smoking, drinking, drugs and now to too many babies. Somehow our cumulative advice is deadening, giving people a negative view of health. Instead could we not say 'yes' to innocent whole-hearted recreational pursuits, so giving a considered, buoyant, positive view of health?

(Roger Bannister, British athlete, born 1929, of sub 4-minute mile fame)

Health has a great deal to do with the quality of our lives. It is an end and a means in the quest for quality, desirable for its own sake, but also essential if people are to live creatively and constructively. Health frees the individual to live up to his potential.

(John.W. Gardner, former US Secretary of Health, Education and Welfare, 1912–2002).

Being fit to enjoy life.

The health of biological man can be interpreted as performance. For peak of performance according to the need, and for the maintenance of health throughout the whole of a long life reserves are needed. Reserves are not provided without effort. The key to bodily wellbeing is the efficiency of the oxygen transport system, which is developed and maintained by regular exercise, and in some cases can even be enlarged. Wellbeing is also dependent upon a high sensory input and maximum cerebral, and one might add now social, is common to all members of the human species, irrespective of variation.

The phenomena of wellbeing, therefore, have physical and emotional components. It is impossible to describe wellbeing in completely objective terms, but the common experience of emerging from the sea on a summer holiday has been used to identify the subjective feelings of wellbeing. There should be no handicap of inner emotional tension, no handicap of disagreeable symptoms, but on the contrary a pleasurable sensation derived from the body itself and from one's lifestyle.

(A. J. Dalzell Ward, author of the bestseller *The Idea of Positive Health*).

And a final definition, linking health to happiness:

Health is closely akin to happiness. If we accept this notion, then being 'healthy' doesn't mean we have to follow food 'fads' or become obsessional joggers or any other sort of health fanatic. Just by slightly altering the way we live, we can lower our chances of getting particularly nasty diseases like cancer

*and heart trouble and add not just years to our lives but years
we will enjoy living.*

(Michael O'Donnell, editor of the *American Journal of
Health Promotion*).

HOW WELL ARE WE? – WHAT DOES 'WELLBEING' MEAN IN PRACTICE?

AstraZeneca's entire business is focused on improving people's health, and our success is directly linked to the health
and wellbeing of our staff.

In the twenty-first century people have higher goals than
people of previous centuries. For example, today we hope
that a job will not only be secure but also interesting and
fulfilling (Terkel 1972); we do not see work as the primary
activity of life but as a component of a rich and varied life;
and rather than seeing family life as forever having to fit
into work's demands we now see the family as the more
important element of life in the long term.

If any organization expects its people to sustain quality
performance over a period of years, and if its employees
hope to have a 'life' as well as a job, then two starting points
must be accepted: first, individuals have a duty of care to
themselves, and in order to sustain an enjoyable life they
need to look after their own health and wellbeing; secondly,
the company has a responsibility of providing a climate and
culture in which people can feel positive and enthusiastic
about what they are doing and have a clear sense of purpose as they contribute to the company's and their own
success.

With these two facts in mind corporate health has
worked with others in the organization on a number of
strategies and programs designed to promote wellbeing
throughout AstraZeneca.

The first goal has been to attempt to define health and
wellbeing. The purpose of defining these goals is to enable

the organization and the individuals within it to have some measure for assessing the boundaries and possibilities for creating a culture, a career and a lifestyle that bring both reward and pleasure. This has not been easy, because defining wellbeing is a little like trying to capture fog with a tennis racquet! Yet there are some broad principles that have been identified for both the organization and the individual – and after outlining these we will take a 'snapshot' of ourselves and look at what wellbeing means in practice around the business.

DEFINING HEALTH AND WELLBEING AT THE INDIVIDUAL LEVEL

A. The individual level

It is perhaps at the personal level that health and wellbeing speak loudest. Wellbeing is hard to define, as we have discussed. It means different things to different people, and, what is more, it means different things to the same person at different points of his or her life (or even week!).

We are probably quite efficient at managing various elements of our lives – our home finances, our holiday schedule, our work routine, for example – but we can sometimes be careless about managing the whole agenda of who we are. We can also be careless about the effect that normal everyday wear and tear can have upon us – the demands of our complex lifestyles, the effects of change, relationships at home and work, the anxieties of living in a world with political unrest and terrorist activity.

Overall, wellbeing is the positive outcome of a number or physical, social, mental, emotional and ethical factors, which will, if they are balanced and in harmony, help us to live happily and creatively. There are four main contributors to personal health and wellbeing.

(i) Self-belief

Dignity, self-awareness, self-confidence and belief in ourselves are essential if we are to respect ourselves and others. This does not mean that we have to think that we are truly marvelous and a major contributor to world history, but it does mean that we should feel comfortable with ourselves and that our behaviors and relationships should reflect who we are and who we are trying to be.

(ii) A balanced life

A human being is comprised of a number of component parts – body, mind, spirit – and wellbeing is greatly aided by having an agreeable balance and regular lifestyle that sustains our physical health, our relationships with family and friends, our need to learn and develop, our emotional stability, our ethical values and our working life and the rewards it offers.

(iii) Time and energy management

As well as being employees of AstraZeneca, we are also members of a family, partners within a significant relationship, parents, friends, colleagues, members of various social groups, enthusiasts for some sport or leisure activity, members of a local community and also individuals with a need for space and time to ourselves. To manage our time and our energy, so that we can play our part and enjoy each of these roles, is one of the secrets of wellbeing (and sanity!).

(iv) A future we look forward to

Having some idea of where we are heading in life can do much to help us enjoy, or cope with, today. Giving time to thinking, hoping and developing enthusiasm for future plans – maybe discussing within the family what we have achieved, what we are currently engaged in, and considering where it might lead; remembering that life is about being, as well as having and doing – all these help achieve a rounded concept of personal wellbeing.

B. At the organizational level

In a consideration of organizational life there are four main factors that can enhance health and wellbeing.

(i) Intelligent leadership

Our work should be well organized, so that expectations and outcomes are clear. The contribution to wellbeing is particularly significant when there is respect for the individual and their diverse needs, where there is recognition and support for individuals and their wellbeing, and when leaders model and encourage effective behaviors in wellbeing, health and work–home balance.

(ii) A positive environment

This embraces cultural as well as physical environment, and includes, for example, well-designed roles that give people the opportunity to make their positive contribution, and be recognized and rewarded. It also requires a safe and comfortable working environment, with resources for social interaction and rest and relaxation at work.

(iii) A focus on health

Health and wellbeing are greatly supported by effective occupational health programs, health screening, fair and efficient return to work procedures, and the encouragement of healthy lifestyles, including appropriate nutrition and exercise.

Individual health and wellbeing is, to a very considerable extent, a matter of personal choice, but at a time, when the sheer number and availability of choices can leave us overwhelmed and confused, some guidance can be helpful.

(iv) Optimum work–life balance

The contribution to a person's wellbeing of family-friendly policies in the workplace – which include maternity/paternity leave, access to places in crèche and nursery facilities, and sensitive management of business travel – is substantial. Likewise, the opportunity to discuss and agree flexibility in working patterns encourages people and organizations to work together toward solutions that are to the benefit of both.

People should assert themselves as human beings by asking themselves questions. If work is dominating life to the extent that everything else just has to fit around it then changes may need to be made. Focusing on getting work done on time is important, but a large proportion of one's time focused on work can, over a prolonged period, lead to a blunting of performance and falloff in output. Sometimes the thoughts of a partner are worth listening to. We all need to build and manage a fulfilling life as well as a successful career. Many of us slip into an unhealthy routine, not by intelligent design, but by slow evolution over a period of years.

It is very easy in today's working environment to be a highly competent accountant, lawyer, research chemist, engineer or whatever, and yet fail as a human being. This is an occupational hazard wherever one works, since most organizations are very demanding.

In the end people have a responsibility to look after themselves. We should not forget that we are more useful to our employers in the long term if we keep ourselves in good shape, not only physically, but in every sense. Repeatedly working long hours can, and often does, result in our losing our creativity, our sparkle and our innovation. And so, rather than honoring our job by giving all those hours to it, we may end up dishonoring our job by ceasing to be the person we were when first employed.

The art of managing our life, rather than letting our life manage us, tends *not* to be a natural skill but an important one to learn and develop if we are to enjoy life at every stage.

STRESS, STRAIN AND BURNOUT

Life is busy for many people employed in the developed world; jobs are often complex. Organizations usually employ few people with serious mental health problems; however, they do employ many who have the potential to become stressed with the result that in addition to any anxiety, or worse, which may result, employees become less productive and useful. More senior staff, in particular, are expected to contribute by being creative and innovative and come up with solutions to problems. It is precisely these attributes and skills that diminish when 'stress', 'strain' or 'burnout' become established.

Although not psychiatric disorders in their own right and not described in the International Classification of Diseases list (ICD-10), these loosely defined lay terms are among the commonest mental health-related causes of impaired work efficiency. They may themselves be harbingers of more serious mental health problems; conversely, they may be the manifestation of an undetected underlying psychiatric disorder. Unfortunately, the terms are used to describe various states of mind and, once again, it is important to establish the exact nature of any particular problems and the symptoms and signs in each individual case.

One observer described stress as 'a reality, like love or electricity – unmistakable in experience but hard to define'. Stress, of course, is not confined to (and often not caused solely by) the workplace but may be related to home life and the social scene. The UK's Health and Safety Executive (2005) defines stress as 'the adverse reaction people have to excessive pressure or other types of demands placed on them'. In the work environment, it arises when the demands of the work environment exceed the employee's ability to cope with or control them. This makes an important distinction between pressure, which can be positive (*pressure cannot be a state of mind*) if managed correctly, and stress, which can be detrimental to health.

All jobs involve some degree of pressure and often such pressures can be positive, improving performance and giving job satisfaction. Where the pressure reaches excessive levels, and continues for some time, it can lead to mental and physical ill health. More information is available at www.hse.gov.uk/stress.

Strain is an alternative term (analogous to its use in engineering parlance) used to describe the consequences of pressure or the load placed on the individual. Stress is not necessarily undesirable. A degree of stress (or pressure) improves performance, and it is only when the symptoms of stress become excessive in either intensity, frequency or chronicity that the consequences become pathological.

Burnout can be considered as the end point in the breakdown of the adaptational process that results from a long-term mismatch between the demands placed upon an individual and the emotional resources that can be brought to bear to cope with these. 'Burnout' therefore results from prolonged and excessive stress caused by work, home or social factors or, as is often the case, a mixture of two or three of these. Burnout and depression share a number of common features and there is approximately

25 percent covariance. The two, however, are not synonymous. Depression is more likely to be associated with fatigue, anergia (characterized by lack of energy), and morbid depressive cognitions, including ideas of guilt, worthlessness and self blame, whereas individuals with burnout are more likely to feel aggrieved and embittered toward their employer. In contrast to depression, the symptoms of burnout tend to be work-specific and not pervasive, affecting every aspect of life, at least in the early stages.

Burnout is more frequently observed in younger, less experienced employees. Other vulnerability factors include an anxiety-prone personality inclined to poor self-esteem and an avoidant, non-confronting coping style. Vulnerable individuals feel powerless to influence their work (and home) environment and perceive an external locus of control in which events and achievements are attributed to chance or to others who are more powerful. This should be compared with those with an internal locus who tend to ascribe events or achievements to their own efforts and abilities. Such people are usually good at influencing and negotiating, with the result that they themselves remain in charge of all, or at least the important, aspects of their lives. Attitudes toward work, such as high or overambitious expectations, are also associated with burnout, as well as certain work-related stressors such as time pressure and an excessive workload.

Stress

As noted earlier, many of the cases of mental ill health seen in the workplace are different manifestations of stress, or, more exactly, stress-related illnesses.

All work puts some pressure on individuals; in general, the more demanding the work the greater the pressure. In turn, pressure normally leads to higher output and satisfaction with work. However, a point of diminishing returns is reached beyond which increasing the load leads to reversed effects – lower efficiency, job satisfaction, performance and mental well-being. Stress itself is not an illness; rather, it is a state. However, it is a very powerful cause of illness. Long-term excessive stress is known to lead to serious health problems.

Recent years have seen a bewildering array of books, magazine articles, television programs and training courses about stress. Some of these can help you find out what stress is, but they rarely give you much of an idea what you can do about it. Stress is best thought of as a series of physical and mental reflexes that exist because they have had a purpose. They are designed to put your body and mind into overdrive for short periods of time, and to help you to deal with short-term crises. It is presumably because they have a survival value that they have been bred into us in times long past.

The problem in the modern world is that few of the pressures that produce stress, so-called 'stressors', can be dealt with by direct physical action – no matter how much we might be tempted by the idea. The aim of quickly getting rid of the stress is usually hard to achieve. As a result we are left with the physical and mental effects of stress over periods of weeks, months or even years, because the stressors do not go away.

Many people feel that experiencing unpleasant stress is a weakness or that they should be able to use their mind or their logic to switch stress off. That is unrealistic; most of us have had the experience of feeling jittery after a 'near miss' in a car, even though we know that the threat has passed and we are completely safe. Stress responses are a set of automatic reflexes that cannot be switched off.

Figure 2.1 depicts the relationship between stress, or pressure/demands on the individual (along the horizontal axis), and performance or output (the vertical axis) – this is sometimes called the 'Human Function Curve' and provides an important model in aiding understanding of the negative effects of stress.

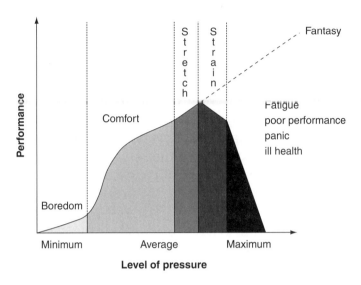

FIGURE 2.1 **Human Function Curve.**
Source: AstraZeneca.

PRESSURE PERFORMANCE STAGES

This relationship can be demonstrated in regard to physical responses to stress (e.g. the changes that can be observed in breathing rate and blood pressure) and psychological performance (e.g. performing mental arithmetic under time pressures), or in terms of group performance, such as the productivity or efficiency of an organization.

Note that initially performance improves under pressure. This is why athletes often produce better results when competing than they do in practice sessions. The whole science of training and sports coaching is aimed at building competitors up to optimal performance for the day of the big event. However, this improvement does not go on forever. There comes a point where performance begins to deteriorate – an experience that all of us will have recognized in others, if not in ourselves. If the pressure is not reduced, then performance is suboptimal and may even lead to 'breakdown'.

21

We all perform at our best when under the right amount of pressure. There comes a point when the pressure becomes too much and our performance suffers. It is important to be aware of the consequences and notice when our efficiency is beginning to fall off. Most people are unable to monitor their own stress levels and are better at seeing them in colleagues, friends or family. Brief overload does nothing more than temporarily reduce performance; major overload can prolong serious illness. Stress, of course, is a normal part of life. The challenge is to manage the pressures so that life is productive and enjoyable.

In an organization (at the workplace), the spectrum of effects ranges from reduced productivity, an increase in errors, lack of creativity, poor decision-making, job dissatisfaction, disloyalty, an increase in sick leave, unpreparedness, requests for early retirement, absenteeism, accidents, theft, organizational breakdown and even sabotage.

In many organizations, only quite serious consequences (those in the second half of the list) are monitored or recognized.

The consequences of stress to the individual include anxiety, fatigue, insomnia, relationship problems, emotional instability, depression, psychosomatic disease, excessive smoking, cardiovascular problems, increased alcohol consumption, drug abuse, eating disorders and even suicide.

THE ROLE OF THE EMPLOYER IN MAXIMIZING HEALTH AND WELLBEING

All organizations want to be successful, all individuals want to enjoy life. How can both these aims be achieved? Figure 2.2 illustrates which points should be considered.

It is commonly believed that resources to deal with mental health should be directed at offering professional support to individuals with problems.

Organization individuals	Poor performance ▲ Progressively worsening *"Health"* state of health	Improving performance Improving health & wellbeing	Excellent performance *High energy levels*
	Support required	**Skills**	**Optimizing performance**

	- EAP etc.	- Task/project
		- Team
		- "Life management"
			• **Work organization**
			  - Role description
			    inc.content & dimensions
			  - Resource allocation
			  - Supportive culture
			  - Good performance
			    management
			  - Flexiable working
			• **Employee effectiveness**
			  - Personal development
			  - Reward and recognition
			  - Work–life balance

FIGURE 2.2 **The role of the employer in maximizing health and wellbeing.**
Source: AstraZeneca.

As with other areas of occupational health, a great many preventative actions can be taken and, of course, the full spectrum of health should be promoted.

In order to ensure that people feel fulfilled and perform well for the organization for which they work, it is important that they are healthy and their wellbeing is considered. There should be a focus on optimizing performance, with proper attention being paid to the way work is organized in terms of appropriate role descriptions, correct resource allocation and full consideration given to requests for flexible working – all contained within a supportive culture that encourages good management of all aspects of performance. All organizations want their employees to be effective at work and it is essential that personal development is encouraged and people are rewarded and recognized for work done well. (Key to long-term effectiveness is an appropriate balance between work and home life, in its totality, *outside* work.)

This should be backed up with appropriate training and education so that employees are, or become, confident and competent. This should primarily revolve around the tasks and skills required, for example assertiveness, team building, leading a project, and so on. Life management skills are important and training should be available (e.g. how to manage one's time, give presentations, learn to say 'no' when workload is high, manage projects). If both organization and training/education are fully addressed then employees should be healthy and be able to perform effectively at their workplace. However, most people run into problems from time to time, and advice and support services should be available – perhaps by way of an Employee Assistance Program (EAP) or, if mental problems are more significant or require specialist help, referral to an occupational health professional, clinical psychologist or psychiatrist.

Much of this effort should be proactive to ensure that employees have the skills to manage the complexity that is part and parcel of everyday life.

A number of definitions of health were used to introduce this chapter. However, clarity regarding what we mean by 'health' and 'wellbeing' is critical if we wish to maximize the contribution that can be made by employees. As Robert Rosen (Rosen and Berger 1991) made clear, 'Healthy people make healthy companies (and *all* types of organization). And healthy companies are more likely, more often, and over a longer period of time, to make healthy profits (maximise output) and to make healthy returns on investments.'

ENERGY

This book is about *innovations* in stress and health and this chapter is posing the question whether management of pressure or energy is the key to high performance. It is proposed that the holistic concept of energy management is key to both improved health *and* increased workplace productivity (Schwartz and McCarty 2007).

Good health and wellbeing is fundamental to the ongoing success of an enterprise. The ability of *trained* leaders to actively mange wellbeing is a critical enabler of such success.

Any organization should be able to realize and release more energy from its employees in order to meet challenging targets and sustain engagement levels. At the same time these employees will employ discretion and are likely to channel some of their increased energy into both their workplace *and* their own enjoyment and participation in life.

Most enterprises are currently experiencing profound change both as part of natural organizational evolution in the twenty-first century and as a result of the global economic situation and recessionary pressures. Organizations need to address not only their employees' cognitive capacities but also their physical, emotional and spiritual health and wellbeing in order to fully gain the benefit of those capacities (Loehr 2007).

Currently, capability training focuses on dealing with people only from the neck upwards, assuming (mistakenly) that 'high performance' relates solely to cognitive capacity. In recent years there has been a growing focus on the relationship between emotional intelligence and high performance. A few theorists have addressed the spiritual dimension – how deeper values and a sense of purpose influence performance. Almost no one has paid any attention to the role played by physical capacities and linked it to cognitive abilities. A successful approach to sustained high performance must capture all these elements and consider the person as a whole, addressing the body, the emotions, the mind and the spirit.

A number of organizations, over the last 20 years or so, have realized that equipping staff to handle the pressures of busy jobs and lives is important. There has been a focus on building 'resilience'. However, this usually allows people to merely 'survive'. What we actually require is for our staff to 'thrive' – to have high *energy* levels, which can be channeled into both productive work and the enjoyment of life.

To be an effective leader of work programs and people, managers must be able to lead and manage *themselves*. They need to be able to accomplish three things to be considered effective – use their 'expertise', demonstrate the ability to 'execute' (get things done) and demonstrate a high level of sensible and positive behavioral performance. The latter has a self-awareness component, for which having good health and a high degree of wellbeing are key. Organizations fostering this approach will increase energy levels.

Some recent research findings follow (Loehr and Schwartz 2003; Groppel and Andelman 2000):

> *Fewer than 15 percent of key leaders in two Fortune 50 companies reported bringing their full energy to work.*

> *Energy was a key component of 'work engagement'.*

> *Energy practices related to beliefs, meaning and purpose, commitment, self-confidence and vision were highly correlated to job satisfaction.*

> *Mental performance and time management improved by 15 percent on days when people exercised, and there was a measurable increase in respect for co-workers, sense of perspective and a better working atmosphere (UK study, 3 major corporations).*

Generating high energy levels is important for all employees but particularly so for leaders, in whom organizations invest a great deal of time and money and on whom, ultimately, organizations depend for their ongoing success. Some executives thrive under ever-increasing pressure although there comes a point (different for everyone) when the pressure becomes too much and our performance suffers. Is the reason for this all in their heads? No. Sustained high achievement demands physical and emotional strength as well as sharp intellect. To bring mind, body and spirit to peak condition, and keep them there, executives need to learn what world-class athletes already know, that recovering energy is as important as expending it.

Employees can perform successfully even if they smoke, drink excessively and weigh too much, or lack emotional skills or a higher purpose for working. *But* they cannot perform to their full potential without a cost *over time*. The cost will be to themselves, to their families and to the organizations for which they work. Put simply, the best long-term performances tap into positive energy at all levels of physical, emotional, mental and spiritual capacity.

- *Physical capacity* builds endurance and promotes mental and emotional recovery.
- *Emotional capacity* creates the internal climate that drives the ideal performance state.
- *Mental capacity* focuses physical and emotional energy on the task at hand.
- *Spiritual capacity* provides a powerful source of motivation, determination and endurance.

(from *The Corporate Athlete*, Groppel and Andelman 2000)

Focusing on these four areas will contribute to increasing employee engagement, while restructuring activity and significant reductions in headcount will most likely put pressure on maintaining high levels of employee engagement.

To keep pace in a fiercely competitive global environment, we demand more than ever from our people. People can easily feel fatigued, distracted, overwhelmed and at risk of becoming discouraged. A number of companies – such as GSK, Sony, Google, Barclays, Unilever, Johnson & Johnson and Toyota – have recognized the problem inherent in the way their people manage their time and, more importantly, their energy levels. There are many examples where addressing this area has led to increased revenues: some of these are described below.

GSK's program is called 'Energy 4 Performance' and Sony's 'Firing On All Cylinders'. The Human Performance Institute and the Energy Project originally provided the training, although in-house trainers have since taken over much of the training in these companies – for cost reasons and to ensure cultural alignment. The employees who attended from GSK self-reported a 30 percent increase in energy levels; approximately 1,000 leaders have now been trained. They also reported:

- a 47 percent increase in the ability to handle work pressure and be more resilient;
- a 45 percent reduction in anxiety levels;
- a 44 percent increase in improved work–life balance;
- a 43 percent increase in perceived communication ability;
- a 41 percent increase in focus

This new-found energy can be used at individuals' discretion, but the company has benefited significantly – sales performance was monitored among attending sales managers and representatives and positive results were shown. Sony also advocates that improvements in personal energy are key to high morale and performance. Over 200 employees in Europe have experienced their transformational program, resulting in like-for-like sales up by 1.2 percent in 2007.

The programs available from The Human Performance Institute, The Energy Project and TIGNUM are very similar. The most effective training is that which is rolled out in workshops spanning three or four days, although shorter courses are available.

Renewal principles are taught via four core modules. These focus on physical (quantity), emotional (quality), mental (focus) and the energy of the human spirit (significance). One-to-one support on nutrition and physical fitness, group exercise classes and the development of energy management rituals add to the unique nature of the workshops, and learning is further sustained through support groups, ongoing coaching and refresher programs.

The programs also focus on ways of working, with an emphasis on distinguishing between low and high priorities, including avoidance of wasting peak energy times on the routine handling of e-mails and not allowing oneself to be interrupted. These workshops also emphasize the importance of organizing work in a sensible manner, including flexible working and planning for business travel and taking appropriate breaks to maintain energy levels, concentrating on the job in hand (e.g. not dealing with e-mails during teleconferences) and completing tasks before moving on to the next.

In companies using these training programs, 75 percent of employees have reported a positive impact on their business relationships.

In AstraZeneca a new global health and wellbeing strategy was supported by the Chief Executive and the Executive Team. This was initially rolled out in 2010 and will reach all parts (regions and functions) by the end of 2015. The objective is to deliver productivity, innovation and competitive advantage by energizing people through global health and wellbeing initiatives.

Critical success factors will be:

- Clear support from senior managers across the organization with active participation as well as endorsement. There will be specific training for senior managers and some will be 'champions', actively promoting a culture of health and wellbeing globally.
- A large percentage of employees become actively engaged in the initiatives; participation levels will be monitored and goals set for uptake levels.

Personal energy management training	• Ways of Working and Living Including 'Perceived Permissions' in the workplace • Movement, Nutrition and Hydration, Rest and Recovery • Mind Matters • Focus on the Future	Talent & Development

Health screening	Available for all employees Follow-up offered	Benefits

Essential health activities	Physical Fitness	Healthy Business Travel	Tobacco Cessation	SHE Strategy
	Healthy Eating	Workplace Pressure Management (inc EAPs)	General Health Promotion	

'Health Connects Us All'

FIGURE 2.3 **An aligned AZ-wide approach to health and wellbeing.**
Source: AstraZeneca.

The strategy will have a framework (Figure 2.3) where **Personal Energy Management Training** will spearhead the drive for improved health and wellbeing. This will be closely followed by comprehensive availability of **Health Screening** provisions – to provide information on current health status accompanied by follow-up where either investigation or treatment of existing problems can be dealt with and lifestyle changes suggested to improve quality of life and longevity.

Finally, as key components in the strategy, **Essential Health Activities** (Figure 2.4) will be promoted.

AstraZeneca is committed to promoting a safe, healthy and energizing work environment in which our people are able to express their talents, drive, innovation and improve business performance. We will do this through activities and incentives that include working with HR, and leveraging opportunities to enhance the wellbeing of our people. We believe strongly that a safe, healthy and energized workforce with sustained high performance will be fundamental to our future success.

Physical Fitness	Healthy Business Travel	Tobacco Cessation
Access to local physical fitness opportunities taking account of individual ability • On site gym facilities • Contribution to external gym membership fees • Align to local / national fitness activities e.g. sponsored walks • Pedometer challenges e.g. GCC • Access to open spaces	**Information and awareness on travel health** e.g. use of services and programs available from International SOS • Travel medications supplied to business travelers including those relevant for high risk areas e.g. malaria prophylaxis • Vaccinations appropriate for the endemic diseases in the countries to be visited • Travel risk assessments • Medicals for employees participating in International Assignment programs	**'Stopping Smoking' awareness programs / advice** • Site 'No Smoking' Policy • Ongoing development of tobacco-free environments
Healthy Eating	**Workplace Pressure Management (inc EAPs)**	**General Health Promotion**
Healthy eating awareness e.g. nutritional and dietary advice • Catering facilities offering healthy eating options • Price incentives for healthy options • Vending machines to include healthy options – preferably at eye level.	**Training programs or support materials on work pressure management including e-learning modules and/or stress management workshops** • Policy on stress management • Stress risk assessments • Work–life balance support • 'Change Management' addressed	**General health promotion with programs linked to local risk factors e.g.** • Heart disease • Cancer awareness • Ergonomics • Infectious diseases • Diabetes • Alcohol and drug awareness • Immunizations e.g. influenza, TB, • Health portal / website

FIGURE 2.4 **Essential health activities.**

Source: AstraZeneca.

REFERENCES

Dalzell Ward, A. J. *The Idea of Positive Health*.

Dalzell Ward, A. J. and Pirrie, D. (1962) *Textbook of Health Education* (London: Tavistock).

Greene, W.H. – Co-author – Introduction to Health Education and Health Promotion, 1974.

Groppel, J. L. and Andelman, B. (2000) *The Corporate Athelete* (New York: John Wiley and Sons).

31

Health and Safety Executive (2005) *Tackling Stress: The Management Standards Approach* (London: Health and Safety Executive).

Loehr, J. (2007) *The Power of Story* (New York: Free Press).

Loehr, J. and Schwartz, T. (2003) *The Power of Full Engagement* (New York: Free Press).

Rosen, R. and Berger, L. (1991) *The Healthy Company: Eight Strategies to Develop People, Productivity and Profit* (Los Angeles: Jeremy P. Tarcher Inc.)

Schwartz, T. and McCarty, C. (2007) 'Manage your energy, not your time', *Harvard Business Review*.

Terkel, S. (1972) *Working* (New York: Avon Books).

WHO (World Health Organization) (1948) Preamble to the Constitution of the World Health Organization as adopted by the International Health Conference, New York, 19–22 June, 1946; signed on 22 July 1946 by the representatives of 61 states (Official Records of the World Health Organization, no. 2, p. 100) and entered into force on 7 April 1948. The definition has not been amended since 1948.

CHAPTER 3

DEVELOPING VITALITY: THE RELATIONSHIP BETWEEN HEALTH AND EMPLOYEE ENGAGEMENT

Susan Cartwright, John Cooper,
Dean Patterson and Philip Gibbs

INTRODUCTION

It has long been recognized that one of the leading causes of death and ill health conditions can be attributed to controllable 'lifestyle' or behavioral risks factors (Donaldson and Blanchard 1995). Factors such as obesity, smoking, lack of exercise, and alcohol consumption have been implicated in the increased risk of coronary heart disease (CHD), one of the major causes of death in the UK. As jobs have tended to become more sedentary, most adults no longer achieve the adequate levels of physical activity essential to maintain fitness and the recommended body mass index (BMI).

While there is much that organizations can do to reduce the health risks inherent in the workplace by changing organizational practices, processes and culture and by redesigning jobs, the workplace, through the introduction of health screening and wellness programs, can also provide the trigger for individuals to implement positive changes in their lifestyle, habits and behaviors. The benefits to the organization of having a healthy workforce are well documented (Cooper and Williams 1994; Cartwright and

Cooper 1997, 2008) primarily in terms of reduced sickness absence. However, in recent years, organizations have increasingly come to recognize that not only is it important to have healthy employees but that they also need to have a workforce that is engaged to perform. Consequently, employee engagement has emerged as both an idea of and a basis for HR strategy (Balain and Sparrow 2009), and items relating to engagement now regularly form part of annual employee attitude surveys.

The concept of employee engagement initially appeared in the academic literature in the early 1990s and was described by Kahn (1990, p. 694) as referring to 'how employees behaviorally apply themselves physically, cognitively and emotionally during (job) role performances'. Physical engagement involves employees applying their physical and mental energies and resources wholly to their job performance. To be cognitively engaged in their work employees need to be acutely aware and aligned with the organizational mission and strategy and know what they need to do to deliver the optimal return on their work efforts; emotional engagement, on the other hand, relates to the degree to which employees feel connected with and trust the organization and its members (Callan and Lawrence 2008). According to May *et al.* (2004), highly engaged employees are able to completely immerse themselves in their work and so consider engagement to be a distinct and arguably a more powerful predictor of job performance than concepts such as intrinsic motivation, job involvement and organizational commitment.

The precise relationship between health and engagement is still not clear (Robertson and Flint-Taylor 2008; Quick *et al.* 2008). In large part this is due to the lack of consensus regarding the way in which engagement is defined and measured (Balain and Sparrow 2009). However, it is reasonable to expect that health will play a role in determining levels of physical engagement and that improvements in psychological health will enhance emotional wellbeing.

The benefits of health promotion activities in improving health status and health-related outcomes have been widely researched (Donaldson 1995); however, there is less evidence as to the impact these activities have on organizational outcomes such as productivity and job-related attitudes such as engagement.

The primary aim of this evaluation was to investigate whether health promotion activities can be a potential means of improving both employee engagement and health.

BACKGROUND

Unilever is a global corporation and market leader in the manufacture and supply of consumer goods. 160 million times a day someone, somewhere, chooses a Unilever product. Its wide and varied portfolio of branded products consists of many well-known household names, including Flora, Marmite, Hellmans, Dove, Sure, Persil and Ben and Jerry's ice cream. As an organization, Unilever recognizes that their food, home and personal care brands can make a positive impact on peoples' health and wellbeing. Consistent with this view, Unilever also strives to create a positive organizational culture in which employees actively think about their own health and wellbeing.

Occupational health has a long history in Unilever and is recognized as playing a significant role in the success of the company. This concern for employee welfare can be traced to its founder, the philanthropist William Hesketh Lever. In the 1880s, Lever built the town of Port Sunlight to provide the employees of his company, Lever Brothers, with good quality housing and sanitation. Lever Brothers also offered favorable pay and working conditions in comparison with other similar industries at that time.

Today, Unilever employs around 170,000 employees across the world. Whereas in some parts of the world, such as North America, the focus is on healthcare costs, other regions, such as Western Europe, tend to focus on the benefits of improved performance and others, such as Asia, on a more holistic sense of wellbeing. However, irrespective of the operating country, Unilever is committed to maximize the health status of its workforce and improve the value of its human capital.

As part of its global program in health and wellbeing, the company launched its Senior Leadership Health Initiative to its top 51 leaders across the business, all of whom received personal coaching in exercise, nutrition and mental resilience over a six-month period. This wellness initiative is in the process of being extended to employees across the whole business through the Lamplighter program.

This chapter describes the Lamplighter program and presents the recent results from an evaluative study following its delivery to office-based staff at corporate headquarters in London. The evaluation focused not only on individual health outcomes but also on the potential business benefits of participation.

ORGANIZATIONAL WELLNESS PROGRAMS

Worksite health promotion (WHP) or organizational wellness programs (OWP) traditionally incorporate a combination of diagnostic, educational and behavior modification activities which are initiated, endorsed and supported by the employing organization (Matteson and Ivancevich 1988; Parks and Steelman 2008; Sauter *et al.* 1996). OWPs can be delivered either on- or offsite and endeavor to reduce or correct health-related problems as well as promote good health behaviors (Wolfe *et al.* 1994).

The WHO (WHO 1946) defines health promotion as 'the process of enabling people to exert control over the determinants of health and thereby improve their health'. Implicit in this definition is the notion that workplace programs should not only assist individuals in address-ing lifestyle-related attitudes and behaviors but also help them to cope better with workplace demands and stres-sors. However, in practice, some wellness programs are confined to providing basic educational advice on smok-ing cessation and good eating habits, while others are more comprehensive and multi-modular in their approach and offer relaxation training, tailored exercise programs and stress management. Parks and Steelman (2008) differentiate between those OWPs that address fitness only and focus on the promotion of physical activity and those which provide a more comprehensive content.

Apart from reductions in absenteeism, staff turnover, early retirement and other medical-related costs, OWPs are also believed to result in increased employee productivity. However, although OWPs have increased in popularity and appear to have obvious benefits, there is still relatively lim-ited empirical evidence to demonstrate their effectiveness, particularly in terms of the productivity link.

The results of a recent meta-analysis conducted by Parks and Steelman (2008) confirmed that employees who par-ticipated in an OWP were less likely to take time off work compared with non-participants and were generally health-ier. Improved physical health has also been shown to lead to improvements in psychological wellbeing (Noblet and LaMontagne 2008), increased job satisfaction (Kirkcaldy *et al.* 1994) and more positive organizational attitudes (Zoller 2004).

However, Watson and Gauthie (2003) have highlighted the variation, breadth and depth in program content as an obstacle to informative outcome research, given the idiosyncratic nature of what constitutes a wellness program. Such concerns are exemplified by a recent large-scale meta-analysis conducted by Conn and colleagues (2009) based on primary studies of wellness interventions between 1969 and late 2007 involving data collected from over 38,000 employees. In combining the findings of all the studies, these results showed that overall the programs produced only a modest improvement in fitness and health benefits due to the significant amount of heterogeneity in the content, focus and outcomes across the individual programs. In short, some interventions improve fitness and wellness, while others fail to have any significant impact and provide a poor return on investment.

Donaldson and Blanchard (1995) have further challenged the value of OWPs in terms of the extent to which such programs are voluntary and appeal only to particular employee categories, attract the 'worried well' and so have limited benefits. They also suggest that that male employees are more likely to participate in wellness programs than females and that fitness programs, because they require a great deal of time and effort, experience a 50 percent dropout rate within the first few months (Dishman and Buckworth 1996). Evidence also suggests that even when participants follow a program to completion within a short period 70 percent of individuals fail to maintain their positive exercise habits in the long term.

UNILVER'S ATTITUDE TOWARD EMPLOYEE HEALTH

However, without doubt, as with any organizational initiative, the success of any wellness program is heavily dependent upon the effectiveness and rigor of the planning and implementation process, with the support of senior management being a crucial factor. The importance placed on health and wellbeing by Unilever is reflected in its mission 'to add vitality to life'. This is a simple statement but it carries a lot of power in providing a focus to its portfolio, its work with partners and its own people and giving a clear direction. When Unilever published its mission statement advocating the value of vitality, the occupational health department took the opportunity to bring 'vitality' to its

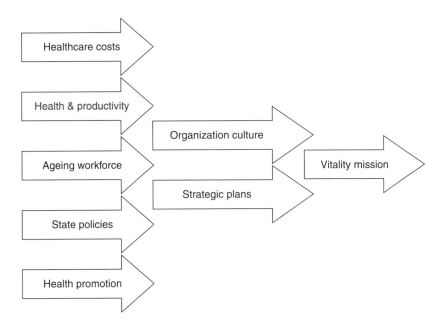

FIGURE 3.1 **Unilever's health initiatives.**

own employees through its health initiative. Importantly, as shown in Figure 3.1) this resulted in the re-alignment of Unilever's healthcare services in a way which makes its health initiatives an integral part of its mainstream business strategies.

BACKGROUND TO THE LAMPLIGHTER PROGRAM

From discussions with staff, it was recognized that, while there were not significant problems of ill health per se in the organization, there were concerns about a loss of energy. In 2001, the company introduced its Senior Leadership Health Initiative, which involved its top 50 leaders across the business. Through one-to-one health coaching, over 70 percent of leaders reported that their overall health had improved and over 80 percent had experienced a significant increase in energy levels. In 2003, this was followed by the

Viper Initiative, which involved 600 people across 3 sites. Again this showed significant improvements in health and energy levels and reductions in absenteeism. The program was evaluated as having produced a return on investment of £3.73: 1 (Mills *et al.* 2007).

This program was further developed to form the Lamplighter Program, which since 2005 has been rolled out to employees working in Africa, the Middle East and Turkey. Again, data collected from participants has shown improvements in a range of biological scores, for example BMI, blood pressure, cholesterol, and the program positively impacted on other lifestyle-related risk factors, for example poor exercise, nutrition and smoking behavior.

In 2009, the Lamplighter Program was taken to another level in a head office department based in London with a view to evaluating its impact not just on traditional health-related measures but also on more business-focused outcomes such as engagement and performance.

THE LAMPLIGHTER PROGRAM

The Lamplighter program has three main objectives:

(i) to improve health and wellbeing;
(ii) to contribute to vitality through better energy renewal and
(iii) to track any associated business benefits.

The Lamplighter Program is based on the model shown in Figure 3.2 and is focused on exercise, nutrition and mental resilience. It utilizes coaching as a key element.

The name 'Lamplighter' comes from the notion of the Victorian lamplighters who used to individually light street lamps to brighten up certain parts of a particular area. In adopting this name, Unilever aims to 'shine a light' on employees' health and wellbeing as well as demonstrate its willingness to invest in its employees. The program focuses

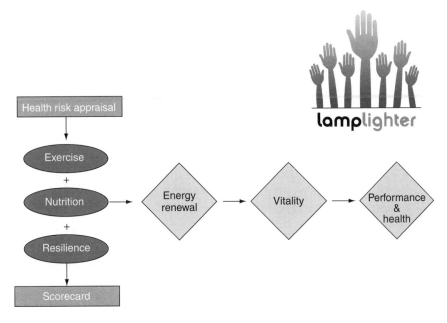

FIGURE 3.2 **The Lamplighter Program.**

on improving wellness through a combination of diagnostic and educative activities whereby individuals work with a team of experts to create their own personal improvement plan. The program is led by the occupational health (OH) department, which conducts health assessments, provides dietary and lifestyle advice and develops an individualized program of exercise. OH works together with Human Resources (HR) professionals who conduct performance assessments of those involved in the program. All the data collected is then evaluated independently of the organization by a research team at Lancaster University.

At the beginning of the program, individuals are assigned a total health score by the occupational health team. The maximum total health score of 170 is based on six core factors. These factors are:

(i) Non-modifiable risk factors (i.e. age, gender, family history) – maximum score = 15;

(ii) Lifestyle risk factors (e.g. smoking habits, blood pres sure) – maximum Score = 25;

(iii) Nutritional habits (e.g. consumption of red meat, fresh fruit, units of alcohol) – maximum score = 25;

(iv) Fitness (e.g. BMI aerobic capacity) – maximum score = 35;

(v) Workplace-related health and behaviors (e.g. engagement levels, performance and pressure levels at work) – maximum score = 40; and

(vi) Biochemistry (e.g. cholesterol, glucose levels) – maximum score = 30.

Participants with pre-existing health conditions, those taking medication or with bone or joint problems were asked to seek advice from their doctor before taking part in the program.

In addition, participants are given the opportunity to complete the Pressure Management Indicator (PMI) (Cooper and Williams 1996). This tool is designed to measure individual levels of pressure in relation to a range of specific workplace stressors as well as assess individual factors such as personality and current coping strategies that may effect the way in which an individual deals with experienced pressure. Therefore, the tool was useful in helping participants to gain in-depth insight into aspects of their lives which may have been causing them excessive pressure and to improve the way they handle pressure. The PMI was handled and administered online by an external consultancy. Individuals were given a unique password and were able to download their own personal profile on completion of a questionnaire. The results were benchmarked against a normative group representing over 20,000 managers and employees from other organizations who had previously completed the questionnaire. The details of this profile remain confidential to the individual, and individual details are not reported to Unilever.

At the same time, there are safeguards built into the process to provide assistance and support to those individuals who present profiles that raise concerns. If the external providers encounter extreme scores, individuals are encouraged to seek help through the services of the Employee Assistance Program, a cognitive behavioral therapist or trained psychologist, depending on the level of assessed risk.

Unilever received a summary of the aggregate results of the PMI. This showed overall that, compared with the general working population, Unilever employees were more job satisfied, more satisfied with and committed to the organization and more job secure. Interestingly, in contrast, findings indicated that employees were generally less self-confident than the working population.

In addition, the OH department administered heart rate variability index tests to monitor physiological stress patterns. Any employees showing red flag signs were referred to a psychologist or Employee Assistance Program for professional help.

In total, 52 employees initially started the Lamplighter Program at Unilever House in London early in 2009 and completed the assessment process (Time 1). Having completed the program, they were invited to attend reassessment. This took place approximately six months after they had entered the program (Time 2). However, there was no repeat of the PMI questionnaire.

RESULTS FOLLOWING THE PROGRAM

(i) Health

Of the original 52 participants, only 38 completed the assessments both at Time 1 and Time 2. During the duration of the program seven participants (around 15 percent) dropped out and a further five (10 percent) left the

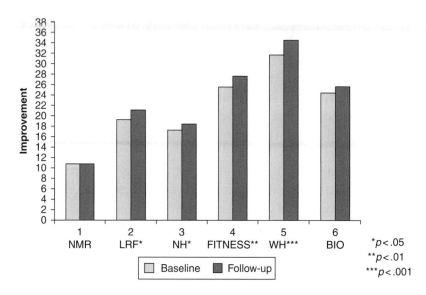

FIGURE 3.3   **Pre- and post-program results of Lamplighter.**

company. Participation in the program was voluntary, and all participants consented to be a part of the evaluation study.

Of the 38 that completed the program, 16 were male and 22 were female. The age of the participants ranged from 25 to 51 years. The results were compared pre- and post-program, and are set out in Figure 3.3.

Statistical analysis performed on the data shows a significant improvement in total health and physiological scores. In particular, lifestyle factors (LRF), nutritional habits (NH), fitness and workplace-related health and behaviors (WH) all improved significantly, with the greatest improvement being in relation to fitness- and workplace-related health and behaviors. The improvement in the total score on the workplace-related health and behaviors suggested that following completion of the program employees felt significantly more engaged with their work, were less likely to take time off work due to health problems, were better able to perform their jobs and less likely to be adversely effected by pressure. In addition, statistically significant improvements were found in relation to:

- resting blood pressure,
- the amount of physical activity,
- portions of red meat consumed per week,
- the amount of fresh fruit, salad and vegetables consumed per day,
- smoking cessation (at the start of the program 24 percent of participants were smokers whereas at the time of the follow-up assessment this figure had reduced to 16 percent).

There were no significant changes in mean biochemistry scores (BIO) or non-modifiable risk factors (NMR). By their very nature, non-modifiable risk factors are fixed and, other than age, do not change over time. While there was a small observed improvement in biochemistry scores these did not reach statistical significance. There may be two possible reasons for this. First, it can take some time for cholesterol, triglycerides and glucose levels to improve substantially. Secondly, participants were rated on a 5-point Likert scale as being very poor (1), poor (2), fair (3), good (4) and very good (5) rather than being given numeric scores that recorded the actual levels of measured cholesterol; these ratings were insufficiently sensitive to reflect the modest yet still significant improvements that were observed.

Results were compared by gender and showed that females had been more inclined to make lifestyle changes than males.

(ii) Productivity and health

The findings provided an evidential link suggesting that improvements in health were associated with improvements in engagement. In order to further test the

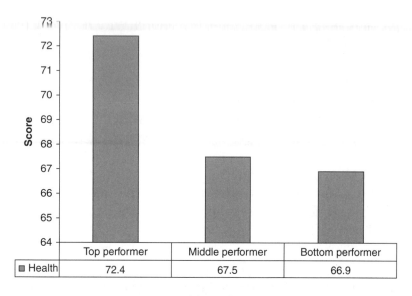

FIGURE 3.4 **Health and performance.**

relationship between productivity and health, total health scores were scrutinized against performance ratings for a sub-sample of 20 employees for whom this data was readily available. This showed that the average total health score for those whose performance was rated in the bottom third were assessed as being in significantly poorer health than their top performing colleagues.

Importantly, lifestyle factors were positively and significantly correlated with both engagement and performance, which would seem to uphold the health–engagement–performance link (Figure 3.4).

Compared with managers/professionals in other organizations, levels of engagement in Unilever were significantly above average.

SUMMARY CONCLUSIONS

The results provided strong evidence that participants in the Lamplighter program gained health benefits. However, the test remains as to whether individuals will continue to maintain the changes they have made in their lives over time. It is hoped that the presence of an onsite gym and healthy food program in the head office building will continue to encourage the positive habits that participants adopted as a result of the program.

Unfortunately, we do not have the data to be able to assess any improvements in the way in which participants deal with any experienced stress, but we believe that improvements in wellness contribute to make individuals more resilient in dealing with the stress and strain of modern-day life.

We also recognize that the positive results we have found are limited by the fact that we did not compare program users with a control group. However, while it is ideal to make this comparison, this often proves difficult or impractical in busy and time-pressured organizational environments.

The study demonstrates that Unilever is fortunate to have a highly job-satisfied and highly engaged workforce and that this contributes to high performance. Programs such as this communicate to employees that the company values them and is committed to ensuring that they remain in good health.

Wellness programs present a way of maintaining and improving the health resources of the individual necessary to achieve optimal physical engagement and performance; but they do not directly address other aspects of engagement such as the need for goal clarity and transformational leadership.

Engagement remains a popular managerial concept, a fact underlined by the assumption that there is a linear relationship between engagement and performance – that organizations should be striving to increase levels of engagement as variously measured by the annual employee year on year – and that performance will inevitably also continue to rise. However, more research is needed to explore the precise relationship between engagement and performance in order to establish whether it is indeed linear in effect. Engagement may not be, as some have argued (Maslach *et al.* 2008), the opposite of 'burnout'; instead it may be that excessive levels of engagement lead to work addiction and have adverse consequences for work–life balance and possibly health. If this is the case then organizations should be careful to ensure that employees are energized by their work yet still have enough energy to satisfactorily balance their work and their lives.

REFERENCES

Balain, S. and Sparrow, P. (2009) 'Engaged to Perform: A New Perspective on Employee Engagement', White paper 09/04 May, Lancaster University Management School.

Callan, V. and Lawrence, S. (2008) 'Building employee engagement, job satisfaction, health and retention', in S. Cartwright and C. L. Cooper (eds), *The Oxford Handbook of Organizational Well Being* (Oxford: Oxford University Press), pp. 411–441.

Cartwright, S. and Cooper, C. L. (1997) *Managing Workplace Stress* (Thousand Oaks, CA: Sage).

Cartwright, S. and Cooper, C. L. (eds) (2008) *The Oxford Handbook of Organizational Well Being* (Oxford: Oxford University Press).

Conn, V. S., Hafdald, A. R., Cooper, P. S., Brown, L. M. and Lusk, S. L. (2009) 'Meta-analysis of workplace physical activity interventions', *American Journal of Preventive Medicine*, 37 (4): 330–338.

Cooper, C. L. and Williams, S. (1994) *Creating Healthy Work Organizations* (Chichester: John Wiley).

Cooper, C. L. and Williams, S. (1996) *Pressure Management Indicator* (Harrogate: Resource Systems).

Dishman, R. and Buckworth, J. (1996) 'Increasing physical activity: a quantitative synthesis', *Medicine and Science in Sports and Exercise*, 28 (6): 706–719.

Donaldson, S. I. (1995) 'Workplace health promotion : a theory-driven empirically based perspective', in L. R. Murphy, J. L. Hurrell, S. L. Sauter and G. P. Keita (eds), *Job Stress*

Interventions (Washington DC: American Psychological Association), pp. 73–90.

Donaldson, S. and Blanchard, A. L. (1995) 'The seven health problems, well being and performance at work: evidence from the value of reaching small and undeserved worksites', *Preventive Medicine*, 24 (3): 270–277.

Kahn, W. A. (1990) 'Psychological conditions of personal engagement and disengagement at work', *Academy of Management Journal*, 33: 692–724

Kirkcaldy, B. D., Cooper, C. L. Shepherd, R. J. and Brown, J. S. (1994) 'Exercise, job satisfaction and well-being among superintendent police officers', *European Review of Applied Psychology*, 44: 117–123.

Maslach, C., Leiter M. P., Schaufeli, W. (2008) 'Measuring Burnout', in S. Cartwright and C. L. Cooper (eds) *The Oxford Handbook of Organizational Well Being* (Oxford: Oxford University Press), pp. 86–108.

Matteson, M. and Ivancevich, J. (1988) 'Health Promotion at Work', in C. L. Cooper and I. T. Robertson (eds), *International Review of Industrial and Organizational Psychology*, 3: 279–306.

May, D. R., Gibson, R. L. and Hartner, L. M. (2004) 'The psychological conditions of meaningfulness, safety and availability and the engagement of the human spirit at work', *Journal of Occupational and Organizational Psychology*, 77: 11–37.

Mills, P. R., Kessler, R. C., Cooper, J. and Sullivan, S. (2007) 'Impact of a health promotion program on employee health risks and productivity', *American Journal of Health Promotion*, 22: 11–45

Noblet, A. J. and LaMontagne, A. D. (2008) 'The challenges of developing, implementing and evaluating interventions', in S. Cartwright and C. L. Cooper (eds) *The Oxford Handbook of Organizational Well-Being* (Oxford: Oxford University Press), pp. 466–496.

Parks, K. M and Steelman, A. A. (2008) 'Organizational wellness programs: a meta-analysis', *Journal of Occupational Health Psychology*, 13 (1): 58–68.

Quick, J. C., Little, L. M. and Nelson, D. L. (2008) 'Positive emotions, attitudes and health: motivated, engaged, focused', in S. Cartwright and C. L. Cooper (eds) *The Oxford Handbook of Organizational Well Being* (Oxford: Oxford University Press), pp. 214–235.

Robertson, I. T. and Flint Taylor, J. (2008) 'Leadership, psychological well-being and organizational outcomes', in S. Cartwright and C. L. Cooper (eds) *The Oxford Handbook of Organizational Well-Being* (Oxford; Oxford University Press), pp. 159–179.

Sauter, S., Lim, S. Y. and Murphy, L. R. (1996) 'Organizational health: a new paradigm for occupational stress research at NIOSH', *Japenese Journal of Occupational Mental Health*, 4: 248–254.

Watson, W. and Gauthie, J. (2003) 'The viability of organizational wellness programs: an examination of promotion and results', *Journal of Social Psychology*, 33 (6): 1297–1312.

WHO (World Health Organization) (1946) Preamble to the Constitution of the World Health Organization, as adopted by the International Health Conference, New York, 19–22 June 1946; signed on 22 July 1946 by representatives of 61 States (Official Records of the World Health Organization, no 2, p.100) and entered into force on 7 April 1948.

Wolfe, R., Parker, D. and Napier, N. (1994) 'Employee health management and organizational performance', *Journal of Applied Behavioral Science*, 30 (1): 22–42.

Zoller, M. (2004) 'Manufacturing health: employee perspectives on problematic outcomes in a workplace health initiative', *Western Journal of Communications*, 68: 278–301.

CHAPTER 4

INNOVATIONS IN HEALTH AND WELLBEING:

MCDONALD'S UK WELLBEING PROGRAM

Mark Blundell

INTRODUCTION

McDonald's is the leading global food service retailer, with more than 32,000 restaurants in 117 countries, over 75 percent of these businesses being operated by local franchises.

In the UK, where the business has around 1,200 restaurants employing over 85,000 people, McDonald's focuses on hiring individuals who share the firm's commitment to delivering great quality and service for customers. This means that, rather than selecting individuals on the basis of their qualifications and experience, McDonald's looks for people with the right attitude.

As a result, it employs people from every age group and every social background. Pensioners work with colleagues who are the same age as their grandchildren. People from leafy suburbs work alongside individuals from inner-city estates. Undergraduates and graduates work shoulder to shoulder with people who left school with no qualifications.

As we shall see later, internal research by the company shows that, across the entire workforce, staff particularly value the vibrant working atmosphere and the sense of belonging that comes from working with this like-minded but diverse group of colleagues. There is also strong evidence that McDonald's customers respond positively too, as the policy is a clear demonstration of the company's promise that 'There's a McDonald's for Everyone'.

To support such a diverse workforce, McDonald's invests more than £35 million each year in training, and over the last five years has put in place a structured 'learning ladder' mapped against nationally recognized qualifications.

Beginning with their Skills for Life program in 2006 and becoming one of the first employers to be given official awarding body status in 2008, McDonald's is now one of the UK's biggest apprenticeship providers and has established a full range of transferable qualifications. These start with a Level 2 BTEC Certificate in Work Skills for 14–19-year-olds in full-time education gained through a structured work experience program, and Level 1 and 2 Certificates in Adult Numeracy and Literacy for those employees who need to brush up on their basic skills. These are followed by a Level 2 Apprenticeship in Hospitality (equivalent to 5 GCSEs of A*–C grade) and a Level 3 Diploma in Shift Management. And finally, from November 2010, it began to offer Foundation Degrees in Managing Business Operations to its Restaurant Managers.

For Jez Langhorn, McDonald's Vice President for People in the UK, the case for this investment in vocational education is clear. Speaking in February 2011, he stated that McDonald's recruitment policy *'revolves around the idea that we hire the very best people from all walks of life based on qualities, not qualifications; potential, not just experience. No matter whether our people are looking to build a career at McDonald's or use the experience as a springboard to a job elsewhere, they want to be able to broaden their skills and knowledge and learn at work. This is clear when you look at the level of engagement with our qualifications program – currently over 16,000 of our people are studying towards national qualifications, 7,000 are studying towards their Apprenticeship, with a further 1,800 having completed it. Over 2,300 have gained our Management Diploma and there have been nearly 5,500 Maths and English passes.'*[1]

'Nonetheless, we run a business and, of course, there's a commercial reality too. First and foremost, in a customer-led business, we need our people to deliver consistent, high-quality customer service in our restaurants. Our work on training and development absolutely drives this though – we've found that if our people are engaged and get something out of coming to work every day, we get far better results. We see improvements in customer satisfaction, staff retention and employee confidence and commitment. That's why, as well as training our people on the smooth running of our restaurants, we give them a much wider learning offer.'

As a result, levels of employee engagement are high. The company's 2010 employee survey found that 84 percent of restaurant staff were proud to work at McDonald's; 94 percent believed that the skills gained at McDonald's would be valuable to other employers; and the average length of service for crew members had risen to two and a half years – with the average tenure for Restaurant Managers rising to over 15 years.

The business benefits of these higher levels of engagement and tenure are also clear. By the end of 2010 McDonald's UK had enjoyed four consecutive years of growth, resulting in an additional £265 million in annual sales.

There are also significant implications for the talent pool within the organization. As Steve Easterbrook, President of McDonald's Europe, has commented, *'at McDonald's, many of our managers and franchisees started with us as hourly paid employees and have grown their careers with us. Indeed, they now run multi-million pound businesses and enjoy commensurate rewards and lifestyles.'*[2]

'I believe that this is a genuine meritocracy in action. Particularly given that some of my most talented people – people that contribute massively to the success of the business – did not have the qualifications or experience prior to joining us that

they would have needed to get even a first interview with many other organizations. Since we can make a hard-nosed assessment of the bottom-line returns we have achieved by investing in these individuals, the case for investing in others is easily made. In short, our business is a meritocracy that changes lives – and I'm very proud of that.'

Supporting Easterbrook's assertion that McDonald's is a *'meritocracy that changes lives'* is a 2009 study undertaken by the Policy Research Institute at Leeds Metropolitan University to formally assess the impact that McDonald's approach to hiring and personal development has had on the social mobility of its workforce.[3]

As part of their study, the Policy Research Institute found that, prior to joining the business, almost half (44 percent) of McDonald's employees had two or more *indicators of disadvantage*: low educational attainment; periods of unemployment; single or no parental figure in formative years; significant parental unemployment; resident of deprived area; long-term sickness or caring responsibility.

More than half (52 percent) of this 'disadvantaged' group had qualifications no higher than NVQ2 equivalent. Indeed, more than a quarter (27 percent) had left school without attaining any formal qualifications. Meanwhile, almost half (45 percent) had lived in areas identified as being in the upper-quintile of the Office for National Statistics' Index of Deprivation at the time when they applied to work at McDonald's.

The Policy Research Institute concluded that *'this research provides ample evidence that McDonald's is contributing significantly to [social mobility]. A good proportion of McDonald's staff are recruited in the full knowledge that they have, in many cases, multiple indicators of labour market disadvantage ... and it is indisputable that the company gives an equal chance to many disadvantaged people.'*

However, as far back as 2008 it was becoming clear to the McDonald's People team that, although the creation of a 'learning ladder' would deliver significant benefits for employees, the business and communities in which the firm operates, this was not a 'silver bullet' which would meet all of the challenges faced by its diverse workforce.

It was at this point, therefore, that the team reviewed the UK business's core People strategy – a strategy based on what McDonald's call the *Fusion Model*.

RELEASING PEOPLE POWER: THE FUSION MODEL

The Fusion Model was initially developed in 2005 as a tool to assist the development of People strategies and tactics, and was the result of the UK People team asking themselves two simple, but fundamental, questions:

1. **What is it that our business needs from our people?** In other words, exactly how does the performance of employees link to the success of the business?
2. **What is it that our people *truly* value about working for us?** In other words, what do employees themselves value (NB: not 'what does the company think they should value' – an important distinction).

The team started with what the business needs and particularly the People elements of the business engine.

To do this they took the well-known Service–Profit chain model as their starting point and, supported by further internal research, found that for a Quick Service Restaurant such as McDonald's it was the '3Cs' – Commitment, Competence and Confidence – which impacted on service delivery and, in turn, on sales and profitability (Figure 4.1).[4]

In short, the foundations of a great customer experience are staff with an *emotional connection* to the business – Commitment. And this Commitment results from every employee sharing the fundamental vision and values of the business, a fact which clearly supports the McDonald's policy of hiring for attitude – 'hire the smile' rather than qualifications and experience.

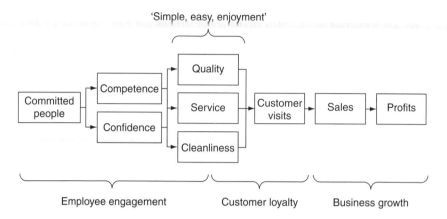

FIGURE 4.1 **The Fusion Model.**
Source: McDonald's.

However, Commitment is largely worthless without Competence – the skills and knowledge the employee needs to deliver the required end result. For example, individuals might have the Commitment needed to climb a mountain, but without the Competence to do so, they will either find themselves either stuck in the car park or – worse – a liability waiting to be rescued from the hillside!

The People team concluded, however, that even a combination of Commitment *and* Competence is not enough, because an individual also needs Confidence – the self-belief to do what they need to do, and to do it well.

So, what the McDonald's business needs from its employees are the 3Cs that drive organizational performance – Commitment, Competence and Confidence. Now they needed to understand what their staff valued most about working for the business. And, once again, their approach to understanding this was very straightforward because they asked their employees a simple question inspired by the company's advertising tagline: 'What do you love most about working for McDonald's?'

In 2005 the feedback to this question was gathered through focus groups in the UK, but in 2008 this same free-response question formed part of an online survey of over 8,000 restaurant staff in 13 countries (Argentina, Australia, Brazil, Canada, China, France, Germany, Japan, Russia, Singapore, UAE, the UK and the USA).

When the total data-set was analyzed by the research team they identified three major themes – themes which were fully aligned with the UK's original 2005 study. However, to ensure that there was no cultural bias in the analysis, first the HR teams in the 13 participating nations were asked to identify the themes emerging from their own country's responses, and then the HR heads of each of these countries took part in a workshop analyzing once again the total data-set. At each stage, the same major themes emerged. These soon became known as the '3Fs':

- **Family:** Working in an enjoyable, energizing environment where everyone feels part of the team.
- **Flexibility:** A challenging, varied job that has the flexibility to fit around a busy lifestyle.
- **Future:** The opportunity to grow and progress by learning personal and work skills that will last a lifetime – whatever direction an individual's life and career may take.

So, the McDonald's People team clearly understood what the business needed from its employees, and they clearly understood what these employees valued about working for the business.

But the major breakthrough had come when it was realized that by bringing the answers to these two questions together, McDonald's had the potential to make the very act of delivering what the business needs something that **simultaneously** creates value for the people who were doing that delivery. For example:

- The business needs a cohesive, focused team, while employees value a sense of belonging.

- The business needs a flexible workforce, while employees value flexible working.
- The business needs well-trained staff, while employees value transferable skills and qualifications.

This is what became known as the Fusion Model, and the creation of the learning ladder described earlier is clearly a direct consequence of 'Fusion thinking'.

2008 STRATEGIC REVIEW

With the logical end point of the learning ladder – the Foundation Degree in Managing Business Operations for Restaurant Managers – already being developed in partnership with Manchester Metropolitan University, in the second half of 2008 the People team returned to the Fusion Model to help shape the thinking for the next suite of workplace innovations.

Their first important decision was that rather than create a program that sat alongside the learning ladder initiatives (and could, therefore, potentially compete with these initiatives for attention and resources), education should continue to form an integral part of the next wave of activity.

This decision proved pivotal in helping to define the challenge the team had set themselves to address: how do we build on the firm foundations of our education programs to (1) ensure the ongoing delivery of the *Future* proposition (one of McDonald's EVPs – Employee Value Propositions) and (2) broaden the scope of reference of our initiatives to further enhance the delivery of our *Family* and *Flexibility* propositions?

The more the team thought about this challenge, the clearer it became that they should be expanding into the area of employee health and wellbeing – and there were three compelling factors that led to this conclusion.

First, the timing was right. The team believed that the successful launch and roll-out of the final education programs on the learning ladder would create the perfect environment in which to broaden the conversation within the business to embrace wider health and wellbeing issues. The internal dialogue could be around 'maintaining momentum' rather than 'starting something new'.

Second, there has been a change in government expectations. Historically, employee health has fallen under the health and safety banner and has been fairly restricted to injuries or illnesses acquired while at work. Government policy was, however, shifting toward a more holistic approach to wellbeing. This shift in thinking has led the concept of *employee health* beyond the workplace to embrace any factor which might potentially impact on employee performance. As a result, the government is signaling a clear expectation that employers should play their part in reducing the burden on public services (such as the increased costs of chronic disease on the National Health Service [NHS]) as well as broadening their focus to areas such as ensuring the security of staff, supporting older workers, empowering young people and encouraging volunteering.

Finally, employees' expectations were also changing, with a general call for greater flexibility in the workplace. It was also clear that staff were beginning to expect services such as improved personal and career development and support, plus a range of health promotion services – all of which suggested a shift from 'work–life balance' to 'work–health balance'.

Furthermore, a review of the literature on employee health and wellbeing pointed to significant business benefits:

- A 'happy and healthy' workforce has been proven to have dramatic effects on workplace morale and to increase retention and productivity. For example, presenteeism (being at work while sick) has been estimated to result in 1.5 times as much working time lost as absenteeism.[5] It has been estimated that for every £1 invested in wellbeing initiatives, businesses typically receive benefits of value £3.[6]

- Employees who are 'well' are physically and mentally able, willing to contribute in the workplace and are likely to be more engaged at work.[7]

So the decision was taken by the team to focus on employee health and wellbeing – the only remaining question being: which areas should they focus on?

WELLBEING STRATEGY IDEATION

The first step was for the team to agree a definition of employee health and wellbeing which reflected the emerging trends outlined above – a definition which embraced the holistic nature of McDonald's commitment to its people. The team believed that it was important that this was a definition which reflected the specific needs of McDonald's business and its people, not a generic 'off the shelf' statement.

As a result, the definition was created in two parts:

First, that McDonald's would be responsible for *'looking after the physical, mental and social health of our people when they are at work.'*

This sets the scope of the firm's involvement – physical, mental and social health – and the fact that as an employer they will take responsibility for the work-related aspects of their employees' wellbeing in these areas.

Second, McDonald's also chose to commit to *'helping employees to help themselves – at work, at home, and as they travel between the two.'*

Not only did the team believe that this was morally the right thing to do, they also felt that there was a powerful business case for this because, very often, wellbeing issues outside work can massively impact upon an individual's performance in the workplace.

With the definition in place, they then set out to identify the key principles for the wellbeing program, which they defined as follows:

- to be inclusive of all staff, but with specific focus on Crew Members (the largest single employee group within the McDonald's workforce);
- to reflect the company's culture and values;
- to provide employees with appropriate wellbeing information and opportunities;
- to capture employees' imaginations;
- to have initiatives which complement each other;
- to clearly illustrate the potential external communication opportunities;
- to maximize the political relevance;
- to be sustainable over the long term.

With the definition and principles in place, the team then undertook a rigorous process to identify those initiatives with the greatest potential impact on McDonald's people and business. This was a five-stage process, as follows.

1. A gap analysis was conducted to clarify:
   - the areas of employee health and wellbeing in which the business needed to be compliant with the law;
   - the initiatives the business currently had in place;
   - the areas in which the business had the opportunity to go beyond the statutory minimum.
2. Publicly available health and wellbeing information from organizations, academic research and government data were reviewed. Based on this analysis, each existing and potential initiative was identified and a rating scheme was devised to assess priority areas:
   - benefit to the individual;

- benefit to the business;
- availability (the number of people that the tactic is currently/potentially available to);
- take-up (the number of people currently/potentially participating in a tactic).

3. The resulting list of potential initiatives was then assessed against a number of key operational criteria, including:
   - potential business benefit;
   - potential operational disruption;
   - cost of implementation;
   - complexity (was the initiative one which was straightforward to explain and to deliver);
   - longevity (was the initiative meeting a long-term need or was it responding to a 'fad'. Also, was it an initiative that the business would be prepared to invest in on an ongoing basis).

4. Employee focus groups were conducted to verify that the resulting shortlist resonated with them and was seen to be meeting the needs of themselves and their colleagues.

The outcome of this process was the identification of eight areas of activity, which meaningfully and holistically address a range of wellbeing issues faced by McDonald's employees both at work and in their private lives (Figure 4.2). These are as follows:

(i) Personal Development
(ii) Financial Health
(iii) Support and Advice
(iv) Flexibility
(v) Physical Activity
(vi) Nutrition
(vii) Personal Safety
(viii) Giving back.

To assist with the communication of these individual initiatives whilst simultaneously conveying the sense of a

FIGURE 4.2   **McDonald's eight areas of activity.**
Source: McDonald's.

'joined-up' program, the People team commissioned the advertising agency VCCP to create a distinctive brand identity for the program.

This branding is used on both the McDonald's employee website, ourlounge.co.uk, and on supporting materials and promotional collateral (Figure 4.3).

Let us now look at each of these initiatives in turn.

i. Personal development: fly

As described earlier, rather than create an employee health and wellbeing program that sat alongside the learning ladder initiatives, the team believed that the personal development initiatives outlined in this chapter should continue to form an integral part of the next wave of activity – hence their inclusion as one of the eight wellbeing initiatives.

Initially this was to eliminate any potential competition for attention and resources between education and

FIGURE 4.3　**Brand identity for McDonald's joined-up program.**
Source: McDonald's.

wellbeing. However, the team quickly realized that the synergies between education and wellbeing were extremely strong, an early example of this being found in the area of financial health.

ii. Financial health: spend

In 2003, a YouGov poll for Insight Investment found that 87 percent of people polled believed money management should be taught in schools.[8] More recent studies support this with the finding that 98 percent of teenagers consider it valuable for the future to learn about managing their money.[9]

However, although there are some opportunities to develop certain financial skills through the mathematics, Personal Social Health & Economic (PHSE) and citizenship curricula, there is currently no coherent money management provision in UK schools.

At the same time, researchers have estimated that 10–15 percent of the workforce are affected by financial problems to an extent that negatively affects job productivity.[10]

As a result, since August 2010 McDonald's have provided the opportunity for all employees to achieve a Level 1 Foundation Certificate in Personal Finance, awarded by the Institute of Financial Services. This is an optional self-study program, which is free of charge to any employee who wishes to enrol for the course.

Furthermore, although the firm is not permitted to give its employees financial advice, they are working with a number of partners including the Financial Services Authority, NatWest and HSBC to provide their staff with information that is independent and trustworthy.

But effective money management is only part of the story – McDonald's is also helping its employee's pay-packets go that little further through a range of discounts with over 1,700 retailers as well as cash-back offers and discounted gift vouchers.

Staff can access these discounts online via the company's employee website, ourlounge.co.uk, and in the six months following its launch in May 2010, 80 percent of staff signed up for the program. By the end of 2010 the firm was anticipating an annual spend through the site approaching £10 million – delivering savings to employees of over £500,000 every year.

iii. Support and advice: know

Initially launched in September 2006 as a channel for online education initiatives, McDonald's employee website, ourlounge.co.uk, has become the central point around which many of the firm's flexibility initiatives are delivered – and it continues to go from strength to strength with over 130,000 registered users (including 50,000 former employees) and over 40,000 visits every day.

In fact on Christmas Day 2009 12,000 people logged on to the site, demonstrating that it has become an integral part of many employees' daily online routine!

In addition to providing access to personal development programs and employee discounts, ourlounge.co.uk also has a dedicated wellbeing portal enabling access to advice and guidance across a wide range of issues. Here staff can access information and support in confidence 24 hours a day, 7 days a week.

The wellbeing portal is highly rated by staff, and in 2010 was averaging over 1,500 visits per week.

iv. Flexibility: live

Flexibility is one of the '3Fs' of the McDonald's Employee Value Proposition, and in the process of developing the EVP the People team realized that people need two distinct – and diametrically opposed – forms of flexibility.

Some employees need **inflexible flexibility** to deal with the big, immovable commitments in their lives. Say parents can drop off their child at school at 08.30, no earlier, and that after dropping the child off at school it takes 15 minutes to get to work. And say that one of the parents has to collect the child at 15.45. It is clear that the only workable shift lies between 08.45 and 15.30. Even a 08.40 start and a 15.35 finish will not do. No amount of persuasion or incentive will change the situation and an employer needs to reflect this inflexibility in the hours it offers this individual.

Other employees, however, need a completely different kind of flexibility to meet their commitments – **flexible flexibility**. It could be the varying demands of caring for an elderly relative, or meeting the fluctuating coursework requirements of a university degree. For these employees a rigid framework would be an obstacle rather than an enabler.

But it is not just commitments that demand workplace flexibility. People's dreams and ambitions need to be accommodated too. McDonald's in the UK employs athletes, charity volunteers, musicians and performers, and countless other individuals with a fulfilling life outside of work. Each of them needs their own personal blend of inflexible and flexible flexibility to follow their particular passion.

This is important to recognize, because flexibility has to be there for everyone. Creating an environment that allows flexibility for one group within the workforce whilst their colleagues pick up the slack would lead to an undesirable imbalance.

McDonald's first iconic move in this area was made in 2006 with the introduction of the Friends and Family Contract – a contract which enables two individuals working in the same McDonald's restaurant to cover each other's shifts with no prior notice or managerial permission, thereby increasing flexible flexibility.

This groundbreaking innovation received the 2006 Working Families Innovation Award, and in June 2007 it featured in the final report of the Equal Opportunity Commission's investigation into the transformation of work: *Enter the Timelords: Transforming Work to Meet the Future*.[11]

This report identified four patterns of work defined by their level of dependence on time and location (Figure 4.4):

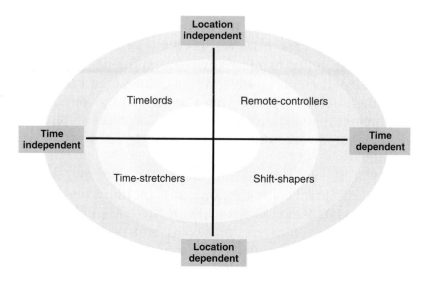

FIGURE 4.4 **Four patterns of work.**
Source: Enter the Timelords: Transforming Work to Meet the Future, Equal Opportunity Commission, 2007.

Applying these working patterns to the UK workforce, the Equal Opportunity Commission concluded that 17 million workers – around 45 percent men and around 55 percent women – could be *shift-shapers*. These individuals, the report concluded, *'need to work in a fixed location, but can have more choice and control over when they work at the front-line or on the production line, which in turn supports employers to be more productive and meet customer demand for 24/7 services.'*

The report also highlighted the experience of identical twins Omah and Ali Dualeh, 22-year-old students who had signed up to the Friends and Family Contract, swapping shifts at one of McDonald's Cardiff restaurants on a regular basis. Omah says:

Having the freedom to cover each other's shifts as and when we need has been brilliant. So far we've used it to help each other out when big course work deadlines have been looming.' It has also made them happier at work and more motivated in their jobs, according to Ali who says, 'We've worked at McDonald's for three years and have always enjoyed it. But having this option has made it even better because we are able to decide who covers a shift ourselves. It shows that our manager values us and trusts us to be well organized.

However, it is important that there are a range of inflexible and flexible programs to suit the needs of all employees. The following are just a sample of those McDonald's currently has in place:

- Restaurant staff are able to choose the hours that they are available for work in advance and their shifts are scheduled within this availability.
- Rotas are operated according to a weekly schedule system, and published ten days in advance giving staff the opportunity to plan and request time off according to their needs.
- Parents can work during school hours with holidays off, while students can work around college and university, often transferring between restaurants during the holidays.
- A part-time scheme for restaurant management is available, which retains both the benefits of part-time working and the career benefits of a management position.
- All employees have access to an online scheduling system via ourlounge.co.uk, which enables them to review and revise their rotas 24/7 from wherever they happen to be and by whichever means.

So, by being both inflexibly flexible *and* flexibly flexible, McDonald's are able to accommodate both the commitments and dreams of all of its employees.

v. Physical activity: play

At the beginning of 2010 McDonald's introduced themed *activity kits* (e.g. 'Spring into Spring' and 'Summer Sports Day'), containing sports equipment and information. These are delivered directly to restaurants and offices three times a year to inspire employees to participate in physical activity, try new sports, and help build teamwork within restaurants.

The kits include full guidance on how to effectively use the equipment and tips on how to organize events (e.g. inter-restaurant competitions, sporting challenges for teams from different shifts.)

In introducing these kits McDonald's had two overarching objectives:

1. To help employees understand the relationship between diet and physical activity, and to provide tools to help motivate them to achieve energy balance.
2. To broaden the EVP's 'Family' proposition by encouraging staff in different restaurants to share details and photographs of their activities via ourlounge.co.uk.

To further support the initiative McDonald's also partnered with gyms and fitness centers across the UK to provide significant savings on membership fees for employees via the employee discount portal on ourlounge.co.uk.

Finally, the creation of a football-themed activity kit in 2010 prompted a massive increase in the number of teams entering the McDonald's Cup. Through the Football Association the firm has supported grass-roots football coaching in the UK since 2002, and the McDonald's Cup is a UK-wide five-a-side football tournament exclusively for the company's employees. The finals are held at Wembley Stadium and following the roll-out of the football activity kit entries rose from 240 teams in 2009 to 650 teams in 2010.

vi. Nutrition: bite

The introduction of themed activity kits also created an opportunity for McDonald's to further engage with their employees around the issue of nutrition.

McDonald's Director of Olympic Sport is double Olympic gold medallist James Cracknell, who the firm have asked to provide its staff with dietary advice via ourlounge.co.uk.

Also available via ourlounge.co.uk are a range of articles (most also available as podcasts) on a range of dietary health topics including nutrition basics, healthy eating, nutrition and weight, food and lifestyle, health and wellbeing of women, and health and wellbeing of men.

vii. Personal safety: be safe

As a 24/7 customer service business, personal safety is an ongoing concern for McDonald's restaurant staff – and in focus group discussions employees express particular concern about traveling to and from the workplace.

As a result, McDonald's has partnered with the UK's leading travel safety charity – the Suzy Lamplugh Trust – in the creation of a personal safety guide to provide advice and best practice on travel to and from work.

McDonald's restaurants tend not to attract significant levels of disorder, but when it does happen the business team are conscious of the distress it causes to staff and customers alike.

Consequently, a conflict resolution training module developed in partnership with Maybo – the UK's leading consultancy in workplace violence and conflict resolution – is now an integral part of the company's Level 3 Diploma in Shift Management.

The company has also invested in a personal alarm system for employees which, when activated, connects the restaurant with a contact center staffed by experienced and professional response operators. These operators are able to speak directly to staff and customers in the restaurant via a public address system and have a trusted relationship with all of the emergency services to ensure an appropriate response depending on the nature of the incident.

viii. Giving back: act

The final area which McDonald's staff told the People team heightened their sense of individual wellbeing was the ability to put something back into their communities. For over 35 years the focus of this activity for McDonald's has been the Ronald McDonald House Charities (RMHC).

The RMHC was formed in 1974, from an unlikely alliance in the USA between the Philadelphia Eagles football team, a hospital in Pennsylvania and a McDonald's franchisee.

On hearing the plight of a young couple whose child was seriously ill with cancer but who were unable to find accommodation near the hospital so that they could be with her, they together established the first 'home away from home'. After the success of the first Ronald McDonald House, RMHC was founded, with the aim of extending this support to children and families who needed it across the world.

RMHC in the UK was established in 1989 as an independent charity which now provides over 400 bedrooms across 14 houses and 29 sets of family rooms, all of which are in, or in close proximity to, UK hospitals and hospices. Families can stay free of charge and for as long as they need to whether it's for two nights or two years.

RMHC's biggest source of income comes from the collection boxes in McDonald's restaurants, through which customers give millions of pounds each year. In addition, McDonald's employees support the charity by organizing fundraising events and donating their personal time.

Outcomes

The starting point for McDonald's wellbeing programs was the creation of a structured 'learning ladder' mapped against nationally recognized qualifications – a process which began in 2006. This has now broadened into the diverse range of activities outlined above.

The business benefits of these higher levels of engagement and tenure have already been explored, but through its annual employee survey McDonald's has also been able to measure improvements in staff perceptions of their own health and wellbeing.

By aggregating the responses to a number of wellbeing-related questions which have been asked every year since 2004 (i.e. before the formal wellbeing program was in place) McDonald's has found that favorable opinion has risen from 79 percent in 2004 to 88 percent in 2010, and as the initiatives which take wellbeing beyond the learning ladder begin to gain traction, the company is confident that this upward momentum can be maintained in the future.

CONCLUSIONS

Reflecting on all of the above, a number of key features stand out as being transferable to other organizations.

First, by truly understanding what the business needs from its employees and what these employees value about working for the business, and then bringing these insights together, it is possible to create an environment where the very act of delivering what the business needs **simultaneously** creates value for the people who are doing that delivery. This has the potential to create very high levels of employee engagement.

Second, by looking at wellbeing in a holistic way, this 'Fusion' of business need and employee value can positively impact on a highly diverse range of organiza tional activities.

Finally, technology, used appropriately, can be a key enabler of delivering wellbeing initiatives in a flexible, accessible and cost-effective manner.

Notes

1. *Adults Learning Journal*, February 2011, The National Institute of Adult Continuing Education.
2. *RSA Journal*, Spring 2010.
3. Policy Research Institute at Leeds Metropolitan University (2009) *Internal and External Labour Markets and Social Mobility: McDonald's as a Case Study*.
4. Heskett, J. L., Jones, T. O., Loveman, G. W., Sasser, W. E., Jr., and Schlesinger, L. A. (1994) 'Putting the service–profit chain to work', *Harvard Business Review*.
5. The Sainsbury Centre for Mental Health (2007) *Mental Health at Work: Developing the Business Case* (London: The Sainsbury Centre for Mental Health).
6. The Chartered Society of Physiotherapists (2010) *Sickness Costs: Physiotherapists Call for Action on Workplace Health* (London: The Chartered Society of Physiotherapists).
7. The Chartered Institute of Personnel and Development (2007) *What's Happening with Wellbeing at Work?* (London: The Chartered Institute of Personnel and Development).
8. http://news.bbc.co.uk/1/hi/business/3261935.stm.
9. http://www.teachernet.gov.uk/teachingandlearning/library/youngpeopleandmoney/.
10. http://scholar.lib.vt.edu/theses/available/etd-10082000-23210012/unrestricted/chapter1and2.pdf.
11. Equal Opportunities Commission (2007) *Enter the Timelords: Transforming Work to Meet the Future* (Manchester: Equal Opportunities Commission).

CHAPTER 5

THE WHOLE IS GREATER THAN THE SUM OF THE PARTS:

DEVELOPING A SYSTEMS APPROACH TO TACKLING MENTAL HEALTH IN THE WORKPLACE

Su Wang, Andrew Kinder and Richard Park

INTRODUCTION

Organizations can struggle to develop a coordinated response to the challenge of mental health issues in the workplace.[1] Occupational health services can seem remote to line managers who need quick advice on their people with stress-related absence. Employees can feel skeptical of the intentions behind wellbeing initiatives. This chapter follows a case study format and explores the challenges that organizations face in managing psychological and mental health in the workplace. It looks at the history of innovation in service provision, and highlights some of the innovative solutions that have supported the psychological health of the Royal Mail Group (RMG). The case study outlines a systemic approach and the role of partnerships with occupational health providers and others to tackle work-related stress through a multi-disciplinary and stepped-care approach. It considers the value of preventative measures, including using stress assessments and education with employees and managers, rehabilitation of stress related absence cases with cognitive behavioral therapy approaches and physical exercise, and the management of traumatic stress within the workplace. Examples are included demonstrating how these have been shown to benefit the organization and employee including cost–benefit evaluations.

Case study – Setting the scene

Royal Mail Group plc. is a communications business in the UK which operates as three well-known and trusted businesses: Post Office Ltd, Royal Mail and Parcelforce Worldwide. Established more than 350 years ago, the organization has consistently been one of the largest employers in the UK. As a service organization, the health and welfare of its employees has necessarily been a key priority and Royal Mail Group has been at the leading edge of mental health support in the workplace for some years.

In 2002 RMG outsourced its in-house occupational health service, and this case study may also be of interest to organizations curious about the sequel to outsourcing. The case history captures serendipitously what happens after an in-house occupational health service, existent for some 150 years, is outsourced, together with the innovations and developments in the more recent nine-year period of managing an outsourced service.

Outsourcing brought its own benefits and also new issues. It fundamentally altered the relationship between occupational health and the organization to that of a contractual relationship. Processes from the former in-house service were carried over and cemented in contractual terms. In one sense, improvements in service provision became harder to achieve. Employee support was still being offered (now contractually) along old lines. However, with goodwill on both sides, developments and changes were achieved.

The success of developments and innovations post-outsourcing gained external recognition in 2006, and again in 2010, when RMG was awarded the prestigious Astor Trophy by the Royal Society for the Prevention of Accidents (RoSPA) for having the best occupational health provision. Again, in 2009, RMG was 'Highly Commended' by RoSPA. Other awards in 2009 included 'Excellence in Health' for its occupational health and counseling/Employee Assistance Program (EAP) services from Business in the Community, and the 'Health at Work' award from Personnel Today.

These awards affirmed, post-outsourcing, RMG's health strategy which put the wellbeing of its employees at the center of its policies. The reader may think that it is easy for large organizations such as RMG to develop innovations and strategy, given its size and breadth. However, competition for resources is a reality, and a stake for budget is required. Steve Boorman, Director of Corporate Responsibility for RMG, noted: 'In the commercial environment of a large organization, there needs to be a compelling reason to provide employee support. Without such then quite simply the money is best spent elsewhere and almost certainly will be!' (Boorman 2009).

FUNDING

Post-outsourcing the Royal Mail health budget was focused on the 'lease and buy back' principle: buying back services contractually from the outsourced occupational health. Funding for innovations in the post-outsourcing years were achieved creatively, through a mix of efficiency savings in the occupational health management budget, working creatively with the outsourced occupational health supplier, and various partnerships with the Department of Health, charities and others. The improvement in morale and better mental health culture achieved indirectly through biopsychosocial musculoskeletal rehabilitation and other physical health interventions are not described here, despite their importance in changing the mental health landscape.

Post-outsourcing, the impact of RMG's health and wellbeing innovations, which included mental health provision, was evaluated by the London School of Economics (2008) in the report *The Value of Rude Health*. The evaluation showed the link between health and wellbeing and improved attendance and productivity. The evaluation showed RMG saved £227million over the three years (2004–7) studied.

The London School of Economics' study reviewed three years' absence data, as well as profitability, cost and productivity measures across the UK network of RMG, and included one-to-one interviews with key personnel, and analysis of employee opinion survey data. The evaluation formed the business case for health and wellbeing in Royal Mail. The study concluded that, if applied to other organizations nationally, there would be a significant impact on the UK economy.

'There is a strong link between both organizations' range of health and wellbeing and absence policies and reductions in absence...Royal Mail Group has demonstrated a highly effective method for improving the group-wide average absence rate...would be worth £1.45 billion to the UK economy' (Marsden and Moriconi 2008).

HISTORY OF INNOVATION

Royal Mail Group has a strong history of supporting the psychological and mental wellbeing of employees. Perhaps the earliest example is the Rowland Hill Fund, created by the Post Office in 1882 as a memorial to the founder of the modern postal service, Sir Rowland Hill. The fund aims to provide practical support for postal workers, pensioners and their dependants in need, and continues to fulfill its charitable objectives to this day.

The Post Office Welfare service was formed after the Second World War to address the physical welfare of workers, for instance instigating the provision of coat-drying rooms for postmen delivering mail on wet days. The role of the Welfare Officers in the early days was to provide advice on issues such as accommodation, debt, childcare and bereavement issues. However, the service needed to keep pace with the changing needs of the organization and the changing face of society. In the 1980s and early 1990s the Post Office was preparing for competition in view of planned deregulation of postal markets across Europe. An internal market was set up for all non-core support services and the Post Office Welfare Service changed its name to Employee Support, and Welfare Officers became Employee Support Advisors. The new name reflected a fresh approach to supporting employees. A telephone helpline was set up providing more immediate access to support, a forerunner to today's 24/7 Helpline service. Alongside this, more formal assessment procedures were introduced and specific intervention products began to be defined for the first time. In essence, the service was 'professionalized' and set about enhancing its social-welfare expertise with time-limited counseling and psychological models of therapeutic support. Recognition of its early innovative approach to mental health can be found in Cooper *et al.* (1990), one of the first studies to consider the impact of counseling services provided in the workplace.

In 1995 Employee Support merged with the Post Office's Occupational Health Service to become Employee Health Services (EHS). This created the possibility of an integrated response to mental health issues with different practitioners now all within one department offering complementary interventions to support mental health and wellbeing at work. During this period one of the Post Office's business performance challenges was the need to manage sickness absence more effectively, with particular focus on stress-related absence, which had grown to rival musculoskeletal problems as one of the two main causes of sickness absence.

Mental health support services in the Post Office (now called the RMG) continued as an internal service within Employee Health Services until August 2002 when, together with its occupational health provision, it was outsourced to an external specialist healthcare organization.

The move from in-house to external provision

In the late 1990s, a business review of non-core services resulted in a decision to outsource the occupational health and counseling service. This decision was executed in 2002. Whilst outsourcing to an external provider has a number of advantages, there are potential disadvantages. For instance, an internal provider of mental health services is likely to offer the following advantages:

- historical relationship with company;
- congruence with company values and goals;
- transparency of cost base;
- in-house knowledge and expertise;
- flexibility.

In contrast, a new supplier of outsourced services may offer:

- cost savings;
- access to wider range of services;
- freedom to concentrate on core activities;
- expertise developed from work with other organizations.

Partnership working

A key to success of the RMG outsourcing of occupational health and mental health support has been the retention of knowledge experts within the organization who actively manage the customer/supplier relationship so that responsiveness is at the heart of the partnership and innovation is cultivated, in the context of a continually changing organization.

RADICAL CHANGE

Historically, Occupational Health and Employee Support Advisors/Welfare Officers had maintained distinctly separate organizational cultures and identities. Occupational Health had tended to be more clearly positioned as a resource for managers to receive advice about an individual employee's fitness for work when experiencing mental health problems. In contrast, Employee Support/Welfare was viewed as an employee benefit, to provide advice, support and counseling to employees who self-referred to the service. Confidentiality underpinned both approaches but the positioning of Employee Support as an employee benefit left the role of providing advice to management largely within the sole remit of the Occupational Health Service. Post-1995, however, this changed, and a new access route was created with the introduction of Business Referrals to Employee Support alongside the self-referral option.

Post-outsourcing this development, which involved a change to the role of Employee Support Advisors, became crucial to the creation of a responsive service providing the pathway for managers to make direct referrals to a counselor or mental health worker, and importantly, to receive reports with an occupational outcome. Line managers could receive advice about work issues, enabling more effective and better management of employees with mental health issues.

Workplace counselors, designated to accept line manager referrals directly, worked to new protocols. Clear clinical protocols were developed for workplace counselors to manage ethical issues in this new role and relationship. These protocols addressed the broader ethical dimensions, which included the management of confidentiality and autonomy between professionals of the outsourced occupational health provision. This breakthrough meant that, for the first time, complex cases requiring time-limited counseling would be provided to the employee in parallel to the occupational health referral, with case management ensuring that services were joined up properly.

From the workplace counselor's perspective, the professional task shifted fundamentally from a 'traditional' model of counseling, where the activity takes place within a dyadic relationship, to one where the influence of the organization was acknowledged implicitly and, where appropriate, explicitly referenced and addressed within the counseling. The three-cornered contract discussed by Pickard and Towler (2003) helped to provide the theoretical framework within which these counselors were trained to operate and work with clients. This model more clearly acknowledges the importance of the systems within which counseling operates.

With a systems approach, mental health provision in an organizational context is not a stand-alone, and other interventions such as mediation, trauma-management services and practical information (e.g. debt management, legal advice or benefits information) are included. These are explored later in this chapter.

A HYBRID PROFESSIONAL ROLE: WELLBEING PRACTITIONER

A new professional role was created to meet RMG's requirements. This new role encompassed elements of roles from a variety of professional disciplines: occupational health advisor, counselor, organizational psychologist, social worker, human resources worker. The core training in the mental health team was in the field of counseling and psychotherapy. The multiple roles adopted by practitioners working with RMG have been reflected in developments in the field of workplace counseling (Hughes and Kinder 2007). Indeed, Royal Mail piloted a successful Diploma Level Training in Organizational Counseling in partnership with the Roehampton University.

Workplace counselors in RMG were expected to understand RMG's organizational culture and workplace factors that might impact on work, and to give appropriate recommendations to line management. Practitioners must be mindful of the different stakeholders involved and be aware of potential conflict between the needs of the client, the organization, the counseling provision and additional parties. Although counseling is a major component of an employee support service provision, the practioner needs to develop an understanding of, and expertise in, a number of related activities, including coaching, mediation, trauma-management services and practical information (e.g. debt management, legal advice or benefits information). To describe more clearly the multifaceted role, a new title, 'Wellbeing Practitioner', was created. The key to this role is flexibility and adaptability. Indeed this is a role that other types of practitioner could fit into subject to any future protected title that may develop in the field of counseling with the approach of statutory regulation through the Council for Healthcare Regulatory Excellance.

SYSTEMIC APPROACH

Drawing on systems theory has enabled RMG to develop an approach to supporting mental health at work by looking beyond the individual parts of the system and focusing on the interrelationships between the parts. As pointed out by Schein (1980), 'organizations are complex social systems; reducing the parts from the whole reduces the overall effectiveness of organizations'.

A systemic perspective helps set psychological and mental health needs within the broader social, political and economic context that the organization is part of, while acknowledging the sub-systems operating within the organization, all of which help to define the experience of individual employees. Within each part of the system exist many sub-systems. For instance, RMG has many thousands of individual employees, each of whom engages with multiple systems outside the organization which may include cultural, gender, racial, religious, political, financial and age-related systems. Within the organization itself, RMG management is structured in a conventional hierarchical architecture with purpose, direction and values cascading down levels of management to the employee. RMG also has an active contract with trade unions which adds yet another dimension to the many overlapping internal systems.

The mental health and wellbeing of employees may be affected by forces from many overlapping social systems, from their own intra-psychic makeup and from within the organization. At the interface between the organization and the individual employee is the line manager. The line manager is especially alerted when work performance, attendance or behavior is affected. Employees with mental health issues are also likely to have active relationships with the National Health Service providers, including the General Practitioner, the Community mental health team, primary care counselors and psychotherapists and/or psychiatrists.

INTEGRATION NOT DISINTEGRATION

A systemic approach provides a framework for understanding the perspectives of different parties. Even in the simplest case when a Wellbeing Practitioner provides psychological support to an employee referred by a line manager, and issues a written report, the Wellbeing Practitioner must be aware of the multiple narratives, and their points of intersection; in this case, the Wellbeing Practitioner, the employee and the line manager.

This approach can, however, become more complex, when professional codes of practice and informed consent are involved. Professional codes of practice also set boundaries around confidentiality of information disclosed by a client. Practitioners must work within these ethical codes and must have the client's agreement for any written report to be communicated to a line manager. Recommendations in these reports should be independent. The employee's and line manager's contexts depend on the nature of the referral and the relationship between them, and may include other personnel such as a second line manager, Human Resources, a trade union and members of the employee's team. For example, an employee who feels bullied by management and has developed depression as a result is unlikely to respond to a mental health intervention that does not address the work issues in a way that will rebuild the damage to the working relationship as well as any damage to the employee's psychological health. The occupational health service has the task of integrating workplace interventions with support provided by the National Health Service. Whether the employee is experiencing intra-psychic issues such as depression or some form of personality disturbance or is struggling with social, domestic or workplace issues, or indeed a combination of all these, the aim is to support the employee through the process of recovery and rehabilitation back into the workplace in a timely way.

EVIDENCE-BASED APPROACH IN THEORY

Royal Mail Group's approach to mental health in the workplace has been informed by evidence of effectiveness (and, in turn, RMC has contributed to the research base available – see Rick *et al.* 2006).

The psycho-social benefit of work is supported by research. Waddell and Burton (2006) conclude in their seminal research that:

> there is a strong evidence base showing that work is generally good for physical and mental health and well-being. Overall, the beneficial effects of work outweigh the risks of work, and are greater than the harmful effects of long-term unemployment or prolonged sickness absence. Work is (our emphasis) generally good for health and well-being.

This should not be interpreted to mean that every type of work is going to increase mental health as it depends on whether in the workplace there are various 'toxins' (Walton 2008). However, it does highlight that mental health can be boosted by work which is meaningful and which gives the individual a sense of purpose.

Although there have been many studies looking at mental health treatments there is no clear consensus about exactly what form this should take in the workplace.

The Department for Work and Pensions commissioned in 2007 a review on evidence supporting approaches designed to avoid long-term incapacity for work. The review (Campbell *et al.* 2007) summarized the evidence as follows:

- Wide agreement in principle that mental health rehabilitation should be based on a biopsychosocial approach.
- Strong evidence that cognitive-behavioral therapy (CBT) interventions are effective for common mental health problems – for example, depression, anxiety. There is also some evidence that:
  - shorter CBT programs (up to eight weeks) may be more effective than longer ones;
  - early CBT interventions are effective;

- CBT is particularly effective for employees with high control roles;
- CBT plus a focus on increasing potential for enhanced control is useful for employees with low control roles.
■ Moderate evidence that brief therapeutic interventions (e.g. counseling) are effective for employees experiencing job-related distress – particularly where these focus on problem identification and solving, rather than the nature of interpersonal relationships.

The British Occupational Health Research Foundation came to similar conclusions (Seymour and Grove 2005).This evidence review suggests that for preventative interventions with populations of employees who are not identified as at high risk and who have not shown any signs of mental health problems, a range of stress management interventions can have a beneficial and practical impact. For retention interventions to help employees considered to be at risk, the most effective programs focused on personal support, individual social skills and coping skills training. It also found that the most effective interventions from healthcare professionals rehabilitating employees back to work involved individual approaches to stress reduction and management as part of a multi-modal programme. The study found that the most effective approach is a brief period (up to eight weeks) of individual therapy, especially if cognitive behavioral in nature, which seems to be effective whether delivered face-to-face or via computer-aided software.

These findings have provided the evidence for developing core and specialist interventions for employees with psychological and mental health problems in the workplace.

EVIDENCE-BASED APPROACH IN PRACTICE

Royal Mail Group developed, in partnership with its outsourced occupational health provider, a comprehensive range of interventions to manage mental health problems in the workplace. These include a core service complemented by bespoke solutions for more complex problems. It is this extensive range of distinct but complementary interventions that will form the focus of the rest of this chapter and can be grouped into the following three areas:

– Business referrals for managers to access advice and commission support for employees, subject to consent and confidentiality agreements.
– Additional Services for additional more specialized or targeted intervention, that is, Bespoke Services.
– EAP for employees and their relatives, to access advice, information and counseling without the involvement of the employer.

WORK-RELATED STRESS: INDIVIDUAL STRESS ASSESSMENT

Over the past 15 years, work-related stress has increasingly become a feature of organizational life. The Health and Safety Executive (HSE) identified work-related stress as one of the hazards of modern working life.

The HSE's Management Standards help employers and employees identify and manage work pressures. Many organizations have internal systems to help managers in the process of conducting stress assessments. RMG created a stress assessment model based on the HSE Management Standards for individuals, termed Individual Stress Assessment.

Royal Mail Group managers are trained in the process of risk assessment and the Royal Mail Intranet Site has guidance to support managers who need to conduct stress assessments. Additional options are available for complex or difficult situations and managers can refer employees for Individual Stress Assessments from RMG's outsourced occupational health provider.

To support RMG operational managers, a simple but key development was agreement by its occupational health supplier that management reports for individuals with work-related stress issues would include the following fields from the HSE Management Standards, which are quoted below:

1 Demands – this includes issues such as workload, work patterns and the work environment.
2 Control – how much say the person has in the way they do their work.
3 Support – this includes the encouragement, sponsorship and resources provided by the organization, line management and colleagues.
4 Relationships – this includes promoting positive working to avoid conflict and dealing with unacceptable behavior.
5 Role – whether people understand their role within the organization and whether the organization ensures that they do not have conflicting roles.
6 Change – how organizational change (large or small) is managed and communicated in the organization.

These reports are termed Individual Stress Assessments and are designed to help managers manage the issues.

STRESS REHABILITATION PROGRAM

In 2007 RMG, in tripartite partnership with its outsourced occupational health provider and an onsite rehabilitation provider, piloted an innovative approach to rehabilitation for stress, based on its successful in-house model of biopsychosocial rehabilitation for musculoskeletal disorders. A Stress Rehabilitation Program, based on the biopsychosocial model, was set up to help employees off sick with stress-related absence.

The model draws on evidence linking physical fitness with psychological wellbeing and combines a series of one-to-one meetings with a stress management consultant with a program of physical exercise provided by a rehabilitation professional. These sessions take place at the employee's workplace and form a bridge back to work in a supportive environment where a structured return to work is expected.

The stress rehabilitation approach is supported by a number of key principles which include:

- Cost-effectiveness – it is likely to be less expensive to rehabilitate an individual after a period of stress-related absence than it is to re-recruit and train new personnel or offer early retirement (Mental Health Foundation 2002).
- Benefits to individuals – rehabilitation can help people retain their jobs and return to work after a period of sickness absence (Thomson *et al.* 2003).
- Benefits of biopsychosocial approach – A meta-analysis of stress management interventions identified that cognitive behavioral interventions (stress awareness and management, perception of stressful situations, health promotion and exercise) aimed at a secondary level were more successful than organizational interventions (van der Klink *et al.* 2001) and a review of workplace interventions for people with common mental health problems by Seymour and Grove (2005), as discussed above, highlighted the value of a variety of approaches within a multi-lingual program.

There are some key differences between the Stress Rehabilitation Program and the model of support provided by more traditional counseling approaches. Prior to the introduction of this new intervention the route for business referrals for stress was workplace counseling. This approach was effective for managing most referrals. However, it was clear that a different intervention was necessary for chronic cases. Below is an anonymized employee quote:

A fantastic experience – it should be used more often –
more people should know about it – it was a great help
(a rehabilitated employee).

BUSINESS REFERRALS: CASE MANAGEMENT

The basic model for business referrals is a case management
approach where a single practitioner takes responsibility
for managing the progress of a referral through a range of
targeted occupational healthcare interventions.

From this initial referral the practitioner either closes the
referral (for example, with advice to the manager about
what may be needed to support the employee) or, alter-
natively, the case can be progressed to another appropriate practitioner for further intervention. This may include
time-limited counseling. When the employee's needs are
more complex and additional resources may be needed,
for example with psychotic illness and illnesses outside the
scope of standard referral, and which require secondary
healthcare, the advice of an occupational physician can be
sought to ensure that appropriate care is arranged and that
the organization is advised of any implications. This was
a new concept of a one-stop shop giving the trusted outsourced occupational health provider the authority to refer
appropriately, to internal professional colleagues. Hitherto
the process was hampered by multiple business referrals.

For mild to moderate mental health conditions additional
resources were available through a portfolio of specialist
bespoke services to target specific areas of concern. The following are some examples of these, which can be provided
on request and are supplementary to business referrals.

WORKPLACE MEDIATION

In the 1980s and 1990s, Welfare Officers would sometimes
intervene in workplace conflict. This might involve 'round

table' meetings where the Welfare Officer acted as an independent facilitator. The development of a team of trained Mediators in the workplace was crucial to take this role to another level and in 2007 workplace mediation was recognized within RMG as a formal intervention.

A report titled *Mediation, An Employers Guide* (ACAS/CIPD 2008) highlights how mediation can have significant business benefits, being both a cost-effective and more constructive way of resolving conflicts compared to the cost of allowing a dispute to escalate to an employment tribunal. The ACAS Code (ACAS 2009) of Practice on Disciplinary and Grievance Procedure (effective from 6 April 2009) expects parties to explore the use of mediation to resolve discipline and grievance issues in the workplace.

Workplace mediation, using the Seven Step Process (Buon 2008), has been used successfully as an intervention in RMG in a variety of situations, including conflict between individuals and between groups within the workplace.

PSYCHOLOGICAL ASSESSMENTS

Psychological assessments are more specialized and in-depth assessments for complex cases. The assessment report is designed to cover issues including but not limited to, post-traumatic stress disorder, cognitive impairment, substance abuse and suicidal ideation. The assessment report advises the referring manager about issues of concern including current impact on fitness for work, treatment options and long-term outlook, together with advice about management of the impact in the workplace. Additional relevant advice about treatment options are provided to the employee when appropriate, and recommendations for additional appropriate interventions to support the individual's recovery and/or rehabilitation are included in reports to management.

COGNITIVE BEHAVIORAL THERAPY (CBT)

CBT, an evidence-based therapeutic intervention endorsed by the National Institute of Clinical Evidence (NICE 2009/2005/2004), is a treatment of choice for mild to moderate mental health problems, including anxiety, depression and post-traumatic stress disorder. Because access to CBT services through the National Health Service is patchy, CBT is a bespoke product in RMG. It has the added benefit that the practitioner is knowledgeable about RMG's work environment and culture.

COMPUTERIZED COGNITIVE BEHAVIORAL THERAPY (CCBT)

NICE (2006) reviewed guidance and endorsed the use of CCBT in specific contexts. CCBT is a generic term referring to several methods of delivering CBT via an interactive computer interface. It can be delivered on a personal computer, over the Internet or via the telephone using interactive voice response systems.

Although not a panacea, employees have found this service effective especially where they are comfortable with computers and prefer the anonymity that the process provides.

TRAUMA SUPPORT

For many years Royal Mail has been at the forefront of professionally supported workplace interventions for employees who have experienced a traumatic incident at work (see Tehrani and Westlake 1994; Tehrani 2004). Dog bites may be the common image of trauma for postal workers but postal workers have also encountered violent crime such as assaults on duty and some have been involved in traffic accidents.

Royal Mail Group employs specially trained colleague workplace trauma supporters as the first-line response. Starting from the evidence-based principle of 'watchful waiting', Trauma Supporters are trained in listening and responding skills and are given a three-yearly competence assessment to ensure that safe practice is followed. Where there is a risk that an individual may develop post-traumatic stress disorder, Trauma Supporters can facilitate referral for professional trauma-focused counseling. This approach was the subject of a long-term research project in which RMG collaborated with its occupational health provider, the Institute of Employment Studies, University of Sheffield and the British Occupational Health Research Foundation. The research sought to understand the impact of organizational interventions after a work-related trauma. The report endorsed the safety and effectiveness of the approach (Rick *et al.* 2006).

SUBSTANCE MISUSE ASSESSMENT

Alcohol and drug misuse can remain hidden in some individuals for long periods. 'Hung-over' workers report lack of concentration and inability to work at normal pace, and they may take more time off from work. Long-term misuse of alcohol can lead to a range of social, psychological and health problems and likely impaired work performance and attendance, leading to increased sickness absence (Kinder and Deacon 2006).

The Alcohol and Substance Abuse Management product provides support for employees attending treatment programs with misuse issues and provides reports to the referring manager about the employee's progress to aid management processes.

BULLYING AND HARASSMENT

In 2003, RMG began work to overhaul its approach to tackling bullying and harassment. Although it had historically been difficult to gather accurate data on the extent of bullying and harassment, a number of factors suggested that bullying and harassment was perceived to be a significant cause of sickness absence. To address this, the following actions were taken:

- A new policy was put in place, together with a 12-step investigation process and a computerized database for tracking the progress of cases.
- All RMG's employees were given diversity training to tackle inappropriate behaviors.
- A number of lay employees in each area were trained as 'Listeners' to provide peer-to-peer support.
- RMG also introduced a free phone bullying and harassment helpline for employees. Available 24/7, 365 days a year, the helpline is open to all employees to discuss their concerns, whether they are a victim, perpetrator or witness of this behavior. An additional feature is that the helpline is provided by an independent provider to ensure that employees feel secure about the confidentiality of the service and that any advice given is impartial.

Royal Mail Group's independent investigators and network of 'Listeners' are supported through Consultative Support groups facilitated by professional counselors, and additional training. In a further development, RMG recently trained a team of RMG people in 'Restoring Relationships' to engage swiftly in situations where interpersonal conflict had developed. This internally resourced approach which borrows from restorative conferencing principles complements the workplace mediation mentioned earlier in this chapter.

PREVENTION IS BETTER THAN CURE

So far this chapter has focused on rehabilitative interventions to support people who have already developed a problem that has affected their work attendance, performance or behavior. However, preventing problems arising in the first place is clearly preferable and so a number of initiatives were developed to help minimize the risk in the form of training courses for employees and managers.

BUILDING RESILIENCE TRAINING

Building resilience is a new workshop influenced strongly by the positive psychology movement (Seligman 1991, 1993). Resilience is the ability to succeed personally and professionally in the midst of a high-pressured, fast-moving and continuously changing environment. Resilience can be cultivated and developed. The training course links personal experience of resilience with additional resources and helps individuals focus on actions to enhance personal resilience.

BEYOND BLUE PROJECT

Traditionally, line management receive training in safety, but little or no training in managing health or wellbeing in the workplace, this being perceived to be the domain of specialists. In the Beyond Blue project RMG sought to deliver additional training in mental health to line managers. The Beyond Blue Depression in the Workplace program is an evaluated and nationally recognized program in Australia with a proven track record, aimed at line managers. RMG participated in a pilot study to test the transferability of effectiveness to the UK. Trained by accredited trainers to the Australian protocol, training was condensed, critically, to a three-hour course. Longer courses would have been a barrier in a busy line manager's timetable. Evaluation of the impact on RMG managers showed overall improvements, including:

- Line manager's knowledge of prevalence of depression doubled from 46 percent to 96 percent.
- Willingness to engage with people with depression and other mental health problems showed shifts of 10–15 percent after training. Interestingly, on some specific questions greater shifts were made:

  'spend an evening socializing with them' (20 percent shift),

  'manage their work performance' (18 percent shift to 100 percent after training) and

  'have that person start working with you closely on a job' (21 percent).

- Stereotypes and negative assumptions – after training, RMG managers changed some negative assumptions:

  'can't be trusted in positions of high responsibility' (13 percent more managers disagreed after training)

  'in high positions of high responsibility should quit their jobs' (7 percent shift to 100 percent disagreeing)

  'are less likely to be viable candidates for job promotion' (17 percent shift).

- Confidence – The line manager's confidence to support, identify and manage staff with mental health problems increased 20–30 percent.

The Project showed that the training increased all managers' confidence on a number of levels, both in terms of supporting and managing staff directly as well as signposting people to appropriate professional help and following this up as needed (acknowledgment: Sainsbury Centre for Mental Health).

COACHING

Linked to the new emphasis on Resilience and the importance of supporting effective line management intervention, coaching is available to managers. Coaching can help individuals achieve positive change in both personal and working lives, helping managers maintain a healthy work–life balance and improved personal performance at work.

In addition to performance or life coaching for managers, RMG has trained a team of lay internal coaches. Recruited from postal grades, workplace coaches help individual colleagues focus positively on what the individual can do to improve personal performance and unlock opportunities for personal development in the organization.

STRESS MANAGEMENT COURSES FOR MANAGERS

Line managers are often fearful of engaging with an employee experiencing psychological distress and can become unduly dependant on 'professionals'. This can link to an increase in cost to the business in terms of sick absence, reduced performance, risk of potential litigation and how the organization is perceived by its employees and customers. Managers as well as employees need training to understand pressure and stress in others as well as learning to manage pressure in their roles.

WORKSHOPS

Royal Mail Group provides training workshops to help managers develop their knowledge and skills. These workshops are designed and run by its occupational health provider. Managers gain:

  a greater awareness and understanding of stress, mental health issues and employee wellbeing in the workplace along with how they can increase their coping resources;

an opportunity to explore the legal aspects of stress in the workplace and to focus on the implications for their work environment and the part they play;

an introduction to stress risk assessments and its practical application in line with health and safety legislation;

development of skills and confidence to support the effective management of employees who may experience stress and psychological issues, including identifying those who may be vulnerable.

Feedback from the workshops has highlighted its value. Of over 300 managers who attended the workshops:

- 85 percent said they had an increased understanding of managing stress in the workplace;
- 80 percent stated the workshop would enhance their effectiveness in performing their role;
- 72 percent saw the course as not only meeting their own objectives, but redefining their values;
- 83 percent felt this was a 'must-attend course' for those involved in people management roles and would certainly recommend the course to other colleagues.

The workshops are facilitated by a stress management professional and are highly interactive with case studies and role plays and use the experiences of the workshop participants, thus providing the ideal environment to explore real-life solutions to everyday situations.

PHYSICAL AND PSYCHOLOGICAL ASSESSMENTS FOR MANAGERS

Recognition of pressures on operational managers has led to the introduction of a structured physical and psychological assessment to help individual managers assess their physical and psychological fitness. Individual feedback is provided together with an overall summary of the management team's 'fitness' to senior management, highlighting general and specific areas of concern and recommendations for follow-up actions. Individual feedback highlights practical steps to improve coping capacity and resilience as well as signposting individuals with specific needs to appropriate sources of support.

FIRST-LINE MANAGERS: BENENDEN

Many organizations have additional health provisions for senior and higher managers, often in the form of private medical insurance. Little, if any, focus is directed to first-line managers. As first-ine managers are critical not only to the business, but also to the care and wellbeing of frontline staff, a special trial intervention, Health and Mental Wellbeing Day, was designed for District Operation Managers and trialed in Cambridge.

The Health and Mental Wellbeing Day was designed to support line managers' physical health and wellbeing, to offer insight into mental health issues on personal and working lives, and to help raise awareness and support for managing staff with common mental health issues, commonly referred to as 'stress'. Physical health checks by nurses for weight, body mass index, blood pressure, random cholesterol and blood sugar were offered. The Health and Mental Wellbeing Day offered mental health information sessions in groups, repeated three times in the day. In addition to group sessions, one-to-one appointments were offered to individuals on a confidential basis. The group information sessions were designed to:

- provide information about common mental health problems (e.g. depression and anxiety);
- help managers recognize signs and symptoms of mental health difficulties;

- help managers talk to members of staff who may be suffering from stress, anxiety or depression about what might be helpful for them;
- give signposting information;
- reduce the stigma around mental health difficulties.

What was distinctive about this intervention was not only the target audience, first-line managers, but the collaboration with a mutual healthcare society, which has been associated with Royal Mail for over 100 years. Many employees of Royal Mail are members of the Society, and this intervention was a new innovation for the Society as well. Feedback from the managers was excellent, with some taking opportunity for one-to-ones. However, numbers are too small for any significant evaluation. The day was deemed successful, and provides a template of engaging with other practitioners, in addition to occupational health provision. Occupational health attended on the day as well.

SELF-REFERRALS – HELP EMPLOYEE ASSISTANCE PROGRAM

Although self-referrals operate 'under the radar' of the organization as a consequence of the confidentiality arrangements, RMG views the unseen benefits of providing access to self-help resources as so important that this service is an essential component of RMG's psychological and mental health support services.

In 2006 RMG extended a pre-existing helpline. The new helpline had a national freephone number, extended hours of availability to 24/7 and provided support to employee and immediate family. It positioned the RMG EAP as a market leader.

The range of issues covered by RMG's EAP include:

- alcohol and drug misuse
- bereavement support

- child and elder care
- debt and consumer issues
- legal issues
- government benefits
- harassment and conflict at work
- health in relation to work
- relationship, divorce and family conflict
- stress, anxiety and depression
- support during organizational change
- trauma support.

The HELP EAP has continued to innovate with new access routes to services and the introduction of a web portal to enable employees to access online information about a wide range of public information. As well as providing telephone and face-to-face counselling the service has also enabled email counseling and is developing other routes of access through web-based systems.

The HELP EAP is a central feature of RMG's psychological and mental health support. A recent survey of users showed:

- 85 percent of employees said the service reduced their anxiety;
- 51 percent said it helped to improve their work performance;
- 96 percent were satisfied with the service;
- 93 percent would recommend the service to others.

CONCLUSION

This chapter tells the history of innovation in workplace psychological and mental health support in the RMG. In reviewing the development of a range of interventions, each with a different focus but each contributing to the whole, the case study highlights the importance of adopting a systemic understanding of the interrelation ships within the workplace and outside the workplace when adapting to changing social and economic conditions and designing interventions to support mental health in the workplace.

The case study illustrates the view that the workplace is a significant part of the employee's life and that supporting individuals with mental health issues is not simply a question of treating the individual employee with appropriate medication or psychological therapy. Successful treatment is likely to be influenced in both positive and negative ways by the employee's experience of work. An effective response to mental health problems by employers can and should form a key part of any integrated social and healthcare policy.

The evidence for success of the overall approach was highlighted at the beginning of the chapter and is compelling (Marsden and Moriconi 2008). It suggests that the sum of the parts is indeed greater than the whole.

THE FUTURE

However, the story does not end here. The current global economic climate dictates ongoing change and a need for continuing innovation to meet existing and new problems. In order to respond to this challenge RMG and its occupational health provider will need to continue to adapt and change if it is to continue to maintain a safety net for the mental health of employees and the organization.

Note

1. The authors would like to thank Dr Steven Boorman, Director of Corporate Responsibility Royal Mail Group, for his committed support and encouragement, without which changes and innovations might have been slowed or not achieved in an organization facing competition for resources.

REFERENCES

ACAS/CIPD (2008) *Mediation: An Employers Guide.* Available online at: www.acas.org.uk.

ACAS (2009) Code of *Practice on Disciplinary and Grievance Procedures*. Available online at: www.acas.org.uk.

Boorman, S. (2009) *NHS Health and Wellbeing: The Boorman Review* (Department of Health).

Buon, T. (2008) 'Perspectives on managing workplace conflict', in A. Kinder, R. Hughes and C. L. Cooper (eds), *Employee Wellbeing Support: A Workplace Resource* (New York: Wiley).

Campbell, J., Wright, C., Moseley, A., Chilvers, R., Richards, S. and Stabb, L. (2007) *Avoiding Long-Term Incapacity for Work: Developing an Early Intervention in Primary Care*, report by the Peninsula Medical School, Primary Care Research Group, on behalf of the Department for Work and Pensions (Health Work and Wellbeing).

Cooper, C. L., Sadri, G., Allison, T., and Reynolds, P. (1990) 'Stress counselling in the post office', *Counselling Psychology Review*, 3(1): 3–11.

Health and Safety Executive *Stress Management Standards*. Available online at: http://www.hse.gov.uk/stress/standards/index.htm.

Hughes, R. and Kinder, A. (2007) *Guidelines for Counselling in the Workplace* (London: BACP).

Kinder, A. and Deacon, S. (2006) 'One for the road?', *Counselling at Work*, Autumn.

London School of Economics and Political Science, London, UK, http://eprints.lse.ac.uk/5148/.

Marsden, D. and Moriconi, S. (2008) 'The value of rude health' (London School of Economics and Political Science: UK), http://eprints.lse.ac.uk/5148/.

NICE (National Institute for Clinical Excellence) (2004) *Clinical Guideline 22 Management of Anxiety (Panic Disorder with or without Agoraphobia and Generalised Anxiety) in Adults in Primary, Secondary and Community Care.*

NICE (2005) *Clinical Guideline 26: Post-Traumatic Stress Disorder (PTSD) – The Management of PTSD in Adults and Children in Primary and Secondary Care.*

NICE (2006) *Technology Appraisal 97 – Depression and Anxiety – Computerised Cognitive Behavioural Therapy (CCBT)*.

NICE (2009) *Clinical Guideline 90 Management of Depression in Primary and Secondary Care*.

Pickard, E. and Towler, J. (2003) 'The invisible client', *Counselling at Work*, 42: 2–4.

Rick, J., O'Regan, S. and Kinder, A. (2006) *Early Intervention following Trauma: A Controlled Longitudinal Study at Royal Mail Group* (BOHRF/Royal Mail/Atos Origin).

Schein, E. H. (1980) *Organizational Psychology*, 3rd edn (Englewood Cliffs, NJ: Prentice-Hall).

Seligman, M. E. P. (1991) *Learned Optimism: How to Change your Mind and Your Way of Life* (New York: Knopf).

Seligman, M. E. P. (1993) *What You Can Change and What You Can't: The Complete Guide to Successful Self-Improvement* (New York: Knopf).

Seymour, L. and Grove, B. (2005) *Workplace Interventions for People with Common Mental Health Problems* (London: British Occupational Health Research Foundation).

Tehrani, N. (2004) *Workplace Trauma – Concepts, Assessments and Interventions* (Hove and New York: Brunner-Routledge).

Tehrani, N. and Westlake, R. (1994) 'Debriefing individuals affected by violence', *Counselling Psychology Quarterly*, 7(3): 251–259.

Thomson, L., Neathey, F. and Rick, J. (2003) *Best Practice in Rehabilitating Employees Following Absence Due to Work-Related Stress* (Institute for Employment Studies (for HSE)).

Van der Klink, J. J., Blonk, R. W., Schene, A. H. and van Dijk, F. J. (2001) 'The benefits of interventions for work-related stress', *American Journal of Public Health*.

Waddell, G. and Burton, A. K. (2006) *Is Work Good for your Health and Well-Being?* (London: The Stationery Office).

Walton, M. (2008) 'In consideration of a toxic workplace: a suitable place for treatment', in A. Kinder, R. Hughes and C. L. Cooper (eds), *Employee Wellbeing Support: A Workplace Resource* (New York: Wiley).

CHAPTER 6

PROMOTING EMOTIONAL WELLBEING THROUGH SOCIAL PRESCRIBING

Hilary Abernethy

INTRODUCTION

Levels of stress within society are increasing – stress over finances and job security has led to a significant rise in the number of patients suffering from stress-related illnesses, and stress levels among UK employees have soared over the period 2010–2011, giving rise to long-term absence across all sectors of employment.

Recent research amongst UK family doctors by Freshminds (2009) for the Family Doctors' Association has shown that 78 percent of GPs have seen an increase in the number of patients showing symptoms of stress or depression over the last 18 months. Job security is the primary cause of stress and of those GPs surveyed, 30 percent said they were prescribing antidepressants to people under the age of 30 for stress.

Over one-third (35 percent) of employers have reported that stress-related absence has increased over the past year and is the main cause of persistently high levels of long-term public-sector absence, according to the latest Chartered Institute of Personnel and Development/Simply

Health statistics. The survey found that 50–73 percent of employers rate stress as among the five most common causes of absence. So how can GPs offer holistic solutions to help their patients address the causes or determinants around stress?

This chapter describes a public health approach to addressing stress, and introduces the concept of Social Prescribing for promoting mental health and emotional wellbeing and treating lower level mental health problems. It will introduce a multifaceted approach to developing resilience – to enable individuals to cope better with stress.

The chapter will offer a definition and description of Social Prescribing and examine how it can be a conduit to deliver resilience-building interventions based on the use of positive psychology, describing an infrastructure for delivery that has been tested in several areas and is currently being delivered in North Lancashire by a range of agencies working collaboratively. They include community, voluntary, educational, employment and leisure services, which are engaged in ensuring that their services are accessible and are supportive of mental wellbeing.

It will also examine the policy context and evidence base for such activity and suggest ways to measure its effectiveness, introducing a common data-set for monitoring and evaluation purposes.

A PUBLIC HEALTH APPROACH TO ADDRESSING STRESS

The Faculty of Public Health defines public health as 'the science and art of preventing disease, prolonging life, and promoting health through the organized effort of society' (Acheson 1988), with its goal being 'the biological, physical and mental wellbeing of all members of society regardless of gender, wealth, ethnicity, sexual orientation, country or political views'.

The modern public health workforce consists of a diverse range of practitioners, and they work across three overlapping domains defined as:

- **Health improvement**: improving health and reducing health inequalities will highlight the work that is undertaken in partnership and in different settings and organizations.
- **Health service improvement** will give examples of the role of public health commissioning.
- **Health protection** involves emergency planning for major incidents such as pandemic flu, the prevention of the spread of communicable diseases and screening programs.

Public health therefore is:

- population based;
- emphasizes collective responsibility for health;
- is protection and disease prevention;
- recognizes the key role of the state;
- is linked to a concern for the underlying socioeconomic and wider determinants of health, as well as disease;
- emphasizes partnerships with all those who contribute to the health of the population.

The determinants of health include all those factors that exert an influence on the health of individuals and populations. These are people's values, cultural, social, economic and environmental living conditions. Social and personal behaviors are strongly affected by the conditions in which people are born, grow, live and work. Figure 6.1 captures the range and complexities of the influences on health.

Public *mental health*, particularly in relation to stress, therefore involves *screening* for risk factors (health

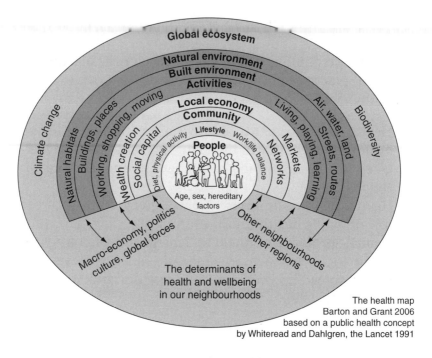

FIGURE 6.1 **The Health Map.**
Source: Barton and Grant 2006.

protection), influencing *service provision* (health service improvement) and *promoting population mental wellbeing* (health improvement).

A SALUTOGENIC APPROACH TO EMOTIONAL WELLBEING

To address the wide range of determinants of mental health, public mental health – and Social Prescribing as an intervention – need to utilize the principles of salutogenesis. This is a term coined by Aaron Antonovsky, a professor of Medical Sociology. The term describes an approach focusing on factors that support human health and wellbeing, rather than on factors that cause disease. More specifically, the *salutogenic model* is concerned with the relationship between health, stress and coping. Antonovsky (1979, 1998) described a variety of influences that led him to the question of how people survive, adapt and overcome in the face of even the most punishing life-stress experiences. He theorized that stress factors are either pathogenic, neutral or salutary, depending on what he called *generalized resistance resources* (GRRs). A GRR is any coping resource that is effective in avoiding or combating a range of psychosocial stressors, resources such as money, ego-strength and social support – they may be internal or they may lie in the social environment, and could be material or non-material in nature.

Antonovsky's essential argument is that *salutogenesis* depends on experiencing a strong 'sense of coherence' – a theoretical formulation that provides a central explanation for the role of stress in human functioning. His research demonstrated that the sense of coherence predicts positive health outcomes.

Sense of Coherence relates to the way in which human agents make sense of the world, use the required resources to respond to it and feel that these responses are meaningful and make sense emotionally.

In his formulation, the sense of coherence has three components:

- *Comprehensibility*: a belief that things happen in an orderly and predictable fashion and a sense that you can understand events in your life and reasonably predict what will happen in the future.
- *Manageability*: a belief that you have the skills or ability, the support, the help, or the resources necessary to take care of things, and that things are manageable and within your control.
- *Meaningfulness*: a belief that things in life are interesting and a source of satisfaction, that things are really worth it and that there is good reason or purpose to care about what happens.

According to Antonovsky, the third element is the most important. If a person believes there is no reason to persist and survive and confront challenges, if they have no sense of meaning, then they will have no motivation to comprehend and manage events. So a salutogenic approach to stress will be twofold – addressing the practical factors or 'stressors' and supporting people to develop GRRs.

DEFINITIONS OF STRESS

Before exploring in more detail how to apply the approaches in dealing with stress, it would be helpful to define just what we mean by the term. The Health and Safety Executive define stress as 'the adverse reaction people have to excessive pressure or other types of demand placed on them. It can be caused by things at work or by things outside of work, or both.' Stress is the body's reaction to a change that requires a physical, mental or emotional adjustment or response. It can come from any situation or thought that makes an individual feel frustrated, angry, nervous or anxious. Stress is caused by an existing stress-causing factor or *stressor.*

Stress has innumerable physical and psychological effects. Two brain components – the hypothalamus and the pituitary glands – lead the charge during stressful events. They release a substance called ACTH (adrenocorticotropic hormone) that stimulates the adrenal gland, near the kidney, to release cortisol – also known as the stress hormone. Cortisol is always secreted in higher levels during the body's 'fight or flight' response to stress. Natural levels of cortisol rise and fall during the day; when it rises our body should be given time so that it can return it to a normal level. Serious problems can occur if our body's stress response is activated too often so that the body does not have a chance to return to normal, hence resulting in a state of chronic stress, including reduced numbers of lymphocytes and reduced levels of antibodies.

The psychological effects of stress are more subtle, but prolonged stress will increase in intensity and if not treated can lead to all sorts of problems such as depression, anxiety and panic attacks. An individual who is under stress will be more quick-tempered and easy to anger and may lose interest in every other aspect of life. People who are under stress tend to find it harder to concentrate and have greater difficulty making decisions. High stress can cause a shortened attention span, less efficient memory recall, lowered objectivity, impaired decision-making ability and other mental problems.

Stress also impacts upon behavior, increasing the desire to smoke, consume alcohol and eat excessively.

Research on psychosocial factors in health by Moos and Swindle (1990) grouped stressors in relation to life domains:

- health stresses and medical conditions;
- home and neighborhood stressors (e.g. safety, cleanliness);
- financial stressors;
- work stressors;
- spouse/partner stressors;
- child stressors (e.g. childcare problems);
- extended family stressors (e.g. caring for ill or elderly relatives);
- friend stressors (e.g. maintaining relationships with friends).

The twofold approach to stress therefore requires providing practical support in addressing such stressors and interventions to increase personal resilience and coping mechanisms in response to stress.

Social Prescribing is a relatively new delivery mechanism for addressing the determinants of mental health in order to improve community wellbeing, integrating this into both policy and operation of new and existing wellbeing and mental health services. It provides a holistic dimension to traditional service models, adds extra capacity to support individuals,minimizes the escalation of symptoms and promotes recovery. Stress is a major determinant of mental health and stress management programs are integrated into the delivery model.

Social Prescribing provides access to non-medical forms of community support to facilitate improved wellbeing. It offers productive, cost-effective and, above all, sustainable delivery mechanisms to achieve success in responding to the challenges of public mental health. Social Prescribing for mental health provides a framework for developing alternative responses to mental distress and a wider recognition of the influence of social, economic and cultural factors on mental health outcomes across the whole spectrum of mental health.

Public mental health focuses on minimizing risk and maximizing resilience. Stress rarely has just one trigger, and the Social Prescribing approach looks very holistically at all aspects of an individual's life and helps them to identify triggers and solutions toward addressing them. The triggers may be external socio-economic factors such as debt, isolation or insufficient support, or internal factors such as poor personal management skills, low self-esteem or low confidence. *The approach allows the delivery of positive psychology interventions, rather than purely focus on a deficits model.*

Potential interventions might include opportunities for arts and creativity, physical activity, learning new skills, volunteering, mutual aid ,befriending and self-help, as well as support with, for example, employment, benefits, housing, debt, legal advice or parenting problems, in addition to traditional stress management education.

The Social Prescribing process has a particular emphasis on empowerment and building self-efficacy. It helps identify the psycho-social causes which impact on an individual's mental wellbeing, and offers practical support to address these. This leads to better long-term outcomes for the treatment of mental health problems, as it focuses on causes – not just treating symptoms. It also builds emotional resilience by boosting confidence, self-esteem and motivation – enabling individuals to cope with risks to mental health in a more adaptive way. The flexible model allows tailored interventions to address diverse needs.

Friedli *et al.* (2009) assert that the long-term aim of Social Prescribing is to improve mental health and quality of life and/or to ameliorate symptoms. Short- and medium-term outcomes include:

- increased awareness of skills, activities and behaviors that improve and protect mental wellbeing – e.g. the adoption of positive steps for mental health;
- increased uptake of arts, leisure, education, volunteering, sporting and other activities by vulnerable and at-risk groups, including people using mental health services;
- increased levels of social contact and social support among marginalized and isolated groups;
- reduced levels of inappropriate prescribing of antidepressants for mild to moderate depression, in line with the National Institute for Health and Clinical Excellence guidelines (NICE 2004);
- reduced waiting lists for counselors and psychological services and
- reduced levels of frequent attendance (defined as more than 12 visits to GP per year).

WHO BENEFITS FROM SOCIAL PRESCRIBING?

Research into Social Prescribing has shown a range of positive outcomes, including emotional, cognitive and social benefits. Broadly, social prescribing is one route to providing psychosocial and/or practical support for:

- vulnerable and at-risk groups, for example low-income single mothers, recently bereaved elderly people, people with chronic physical illness and newly arrived communities (who would all be at risk of experiencing stress);
- people with mild to moderate depression and anxiety;
- people with long-term and enduring mental health problems;
- frequent attenders in primary care (where often stress is a contributing; factor) (Frasure-Smith 2000; Greene 2000; Harris *et al.* 1999).

Vulnerable or at-risk groups

This includes people who are experiencing the worst social and health inequalities. Social Prescribing can help strengthen psychosocial, life and coping skills of individuals, through interventions designed to promote self-efficacy and self-esteem, opportunities to learn new skills and stress/anger/anxiety management and relaxation. Such interventions might include referral to community education groups (such as the Moving Forward Group), referral to arts or learning activity or physical exercise groups, referral to self-help groups or resources such as reading or computerized CBT (CCBT) groups or bibliotherapy (a description of interventions will be given later in the chapter).

People with mild to moderate depression and anxiety

The NICE (2004b) states that *'a focus on symptoms alone is not sufficient because a wide range of biological, psychological and social factors have a significant impact on response to treatment and are not captured by the current diagnostic systems.'*

This recognizes that stressors play an important factor in depression and anxiety and must be considered when planning treatment. Social Prescribing fits well into the 'Stepped Care Approach to Depression' outlined in the NICE guidance, which is a system for delivering and monitoring treatment with the explicit aim of providing the most effective yet lowest intensity treatment to the patient first, and if a person does not benefit from an initial intervention they are 'stepped up' to a more complex intervention. Within the delivery model outlined in the guidance Social Prescribing can provide all the interventions in Steps 1 and 2 and support more intense clinical interventions in the upper steps.

People with long-term and enduring mental health problems

The Department of Health (2006, 2007) strongly advocate a recovery-oriented approach to wellbeing services, with policies asserting that commissioning should be focused on implementing services that are sensitive to individual needs, enable people to maintain their independence, and promote inclusion and the development of social capital (Falzer 2007).

Frequent attenders in primary care

Frequent attenders in primary care are characterized by high rates of psychological distress and social problems, and account for considerable costs in investigatory procedures for medically unexplained symptoms (Karlsson *et al.* 1997), and advocated psychological support. Kersnik identified that frequent attenders were more likely to have lower educational status, were more satisfied with their practitioner and had higher scores of anxiety and depression and lower perceived quality of life (Kersnik *et al.* 2001). Addressing social determinants and increasing personal resources and self-efficacy via Social Prescribing can have considerable impact. An estimated 30 percent of GP consultations have an underlying mental health cause, many of which have a socioeconomic basis, for example debt, family breakdown, trauma, bullying at work and so on. A standard GP consultation does not allow for all these issues to be explored and addressed, so promoting referral from primary care to social, psychological and occupational professionals could therefore be useful to both GPs and patients: individuals would benefit from earlier and more effective treatments; GPs would have fewer repeat visits and there could be net savings to the care budget.

POLICY CONTEXT

November 2010 saw the publication of a new Public Health White Paper, *Healthy Lives, Healthy People: Our Strategy for Public Health in England,* which outlines a radical shift in tackling public health challenges. It recognizes the considerable prevalence in lifestyle-driven health problems, and the degree to which poor levels of mental health in the population impact on that. It also highlights the importance in addressing the increasing gap in health inequalities between rich and poor.

The White Paper adopts a life course framework for tackling the wider social determinants of health with an emphasis on building people's self-esteem, confidence and resilience, and advocates more personalized, preventive services.

The approach outlined in the paper takes a coherent approach to different stages of life and key transitions instead of tackling individual risk factors in isolation. Mental health will be a key element.

As identified in the White Paper, Public mental health interventions cannot ignore the impact on society of health inequalities. There are huge disparities between sections of society in achieving their maximum ability to function, which primarily affects the most deprived and vulnerable and those in minorities and rural remote populations.

The Marmot report (2010) provided a strategic review of health inequalities in England post-2010 and highlighted that people living in the poorest neighborhoods, will, on average, die seven years earlier than people living in the richest neighborhoods. Even more disturbing is that the average difference in disability-free life expectancy is 17 years. So, people in poorer areas not only die sooner, but they will also spend more of their shorter lives with a disability. To illustrate the importance of the gradient, even excluding the poorest five percent and the richest five percent, the gap in life expectancy between low and high income is six years, and the gap in disability-free life expectancy is 13 years.

Marmot identified action on six policy objectives required to reduce health inequalities:

- give every child the best start in life;
- enable all children, young people and adults to maximize their capabilities and have control over their lives;
- create fair employment and good work for all;
- ensure healthy standard of living for all;
- create and develop healthy and sustainable places and communities
- strengthen the role and impact of ill-health prevention.

Fryers *et al.* (2003) identified an inverse relationship between social position and common mental disorders, with those less privileged – with poor education, employment and material circumstances – at increased risk of poor mental health. Other research has also identified that people living in deprived areas and remote rural districts have the highest levels of mental health problems (Melzer *et al.* 2004; Office for National Statistics 2001).

Implementation of Social Prescribing was supported by the recommendations in the Darzi Report, *High Quality Care for All* (Department of Health 2008), which called for the future NHS to focus on promoting health and ensure easier access to quality services. The rhetoric of the public health White Paper indicates that the Coalition Government seems to be echoing this view.

The Darzi Report identified as an immediate step that every locality should commission comprehensive wellbeing and prevention services to improve people's mental health, personalized to meet the specific needs of the local population. It also emphasized engagement with local authorities and the third sector, which again resonates with coalition government plans for both the future of public health and the plans they have laid out regarding the Big Society, as did the focus on increased choice, control and empowerment; and the innovation in service delivery services and a strong focus on outcomes.

The commissioning of Social Prescribing supports the following elements of *High Quality Care for All*:

- delivery of wellbeing and prevention services;
- tailor-made, personalized interventions that meet individual needs and circumstances and promote increased self-management of mental ill health and control over making healthy choices;
- ability to be incorporated into personalized care plans for patients with long-term conditions in order to improve their wellbeing;
- increase in the range of services available, and increased access;
- incorporation of vocational advice that will support people in staying healthy at work and returning to work;
- support for GPs in helping individuals and their families to stay healthy;
- facilitating a partnership approach with the local authority and third sector, enabling mixed-market delivery; and

- tackling the determinants of health (including wider determinants), which enables a health outcomes focus.

A framework for developing emotional wellbeing entitled *Confident Communities, Brighter Futures* (Department of Health 2010) was published in early 2010. The underpinning definition of wellbeing within the document is 'a positive state of mind and body, feeling safe and able to cope, with a sense of connection with people, communities and the wider environment.'

This framework recognizes the need for a systematic multi-agency approach to addressing wellbeing, with key underlying principles, including:

- prioritization of wellbeing;
- a clear strategic approach;
- evidence-based service models and interventions;
- achievement of outcome measures through leadership, multi-agency commissioning and increased skill and capacity in the workforce.

Models of Social Prescribing can offer an infrastructure in which to embed these principles, reflecting the set of dimensions to wellbeing identified within the framework:

- Using a life-course approach to ensure a positive start in life and healthy adult and older years. With such an approach, people develop and share skills to *continue learning* and have *positive social relationships* throughout life.
- Build strength, safety and resilience: *address inequalities* and ensure *safety and security* at individual, relationship, community and environmental levels.
- Develop sustainable, connected communities: create socially inclusive communities that promote *social networks* and *environmental engagement*.

- Integrate physical and mental health: develop *a holistic view of wellbeing* that encompasses both physical and mental health, reduce health-risk behaviour and *promote physical activity.*
- Promote purpose and participation to enhance positive wellbeing through a balance of physical and mental activity, relaxation, generating a positive outlook, *creativity* and *purposeful community activity.*

The Big Society was launched by the coalition government in July 2010 with the aim of 'creating' a climate that empowers local people and communities, building a big society that will 'take power away from politicians and give it to people'. The main priorities are to:

1. **Give communities more powers** – possibilities of communities taking over local facilities and services; recruiting community organizers to build networks and drive action – with a concentration in areas of highest deprivation to tackle inequalities.
2. **Encourage people to take an active role in their communities** – by volunteering; charitable giving and a National Citizen Service for 16-year-olds.
3. **Transfer power from central to local government** – devolution of power and financial responsibility.
4. **Support co-ops, mutuals, charities and social enterprises** – aiming to increase number and the role of such organizations in providing public services – using a transition fund to support capacity building.
5. **Publish government data** – aiming for greater transparency in both spending and performance of public organizations.

The expectation is that implementation of Big Society will increase community participation and build social capital and therefore increase wellbeing via reduced isolation, stronger social ties and greater resilience. Social Prescribing fits well within this model – with its emphasis on partnership work, voluntary sector delivery, volunteering and resilience building.

Another pivotal report in the evidence base for emotional wellbeing is *The Foresight Mental Capital and Wellbeing Project* (2008), which identified major challenges and uncertainties in the future, with two consistent emerging themes: considerable vulnerability of our mental resources and mental wellbeing to those challenges; but on the other hand, the potential of those same resources to adapt and meet those challenges, and indeed to thrive.

The report found that positive mental health and wellbeing were associated with a range of social, economic and health benefits – such as improved education attainment, greater productivity, improved quality of life and social connectedness, reduced crime and risk-taking behavior. A range of determinants were found to be associated with wellbeing and mental health, including strong social support, socioeconomic factors, work or other purposeful activity, self-esteem and autonomy, emotional literacy and physical health. Supporting the development of these factors is a key component of Social Prescribing – with an outcome of building individual resilience.

The report outlines a series of interventions which can all be supported by Social Prescribing and will help build resilience against stress – and increase mental capital and wellbeing. These include interventions to promote personal, family and relationship resilience; promotion of purpose and participation; increased financial literacy – money and debt management and increased employment.

The Centre for Wellbeing at the New Economic Foundation (NEF), London, was commissioned by the Foresight team to research and develop a set of five evidence-based actions that, if practiced regularly, can improve personal wellbeing.

The research showed that despite the financial crisis, once basic needs are met, taking time to develop connections with the world and people around us leads to happier, more fulfilled lives.

THE FIVE WAYS TO WELLBEING

The *five ways to wellbeing* are as follows.

Connect

Connect with the people around you. With family, friends, colleagues and neighbors. At home, work, school or in your local community. Think of these as the cornerstones of your life and invest time in developing them. Building these connections will support and enrich you every day.

Be active

Go for a walk or run. Step outside. Cycle. Play a game. Garden. Dance. Exercising makes you feel good. Most importantly, discover a physical activity you enjoy and one that suits your level of mobility and fitness.

Take notice

Be curious. Catch sight of the beautiful. Remark on the unusual. Notice the changing seasons. Savour the moment, whether you are walking to work, eating lunch or talking to friends. Be aware of the world around you and what you are feeling. Reflecting on your experiences will help you appreciate what matters to you.

Keep learning

Try something new. Rediscover an old interest. Sign up for that course. Take on a different responsibility at work. Fix a bike. Learn to play an instrument or how to cook your favourite food. Set a challenge you will enjoy achieving. Learning new things will make you more confident, as well as being fun.

Give

Do something nice for a friend, or a stranger. Thank someone. Smile. Volunteer your time. Join a community group. Look out, as well as in. Seeing yourself, and your happiness, linked to the wider community can be incredibly rewarding and will create connections with the people around you.

Interventions within a Social Prescribing program can offer support in achieving each of the five ways.

The five ways to wellbeing form an integral part of a new proposal to address inequalities in the northwest of England. 'Living Well' is a new approach for public, private, social and voluntary organizations to work collaboratively to tackle the barriers to wellbeing and reduce inequalities. It involves building on strengths, assets and resilience of individuals and communities to influence change. The key actions for local bodies are:

- sign up to the Living Well approach;
- model the Living Well approach in decision-making;
- promote understanding of Living Well and the concepts of investing for health and delivering social value among staff and with partners;
- use existing powers to the full for the Living Well agenda;
- assess and build on community assets;
- adopt area-based approaches to deliver improvements;
- communicate the five ways to wellbeing to staff and the public and engage people in taking action.

One of the methods of engaging with a wide range of stakeholders in addressing the social determinants of wellbeing and tackling stress was Mental Wellbeing Impact Assessment (MWIA). This is a pioneering methodology that enables a wide range of organizations and programs to understand their impact on mental wellbeing and exists to help build healthy public policy

The MWIA toolkit provides a structured, evidence-based analysis of how policies, proposals, programs and projects might influence mental health and wellbeing, based on four key evidence-based factors which promote and protect mental wellbeing:

- enhancing control,
- increasing resilience and community assets,
- facilitating participation,
- promoting inclusion.

(*Making it Happen*, Department of Health 2001)

The aim of MWIA is to maximize positive and mitigate negative impacts on mental health and wellbeing, focusing on population groups who may experience health inequalities and social injustice and with a particular emphasis on those most at risk of poorer mental wellbeing. It also makes the link with social determinants and helps develop indicators to measure the actual impacts over time.

Using a salutogenic approach, it takes the user through a systematic process of gaining a greater, shared understanding of mental health and wellbeing and its determinants, of identifying action to address the most significant impacts on mental wellbeing that their proposal may have and of developing localized indicators. It has also been a helpful aid as a means to facilitate dialogue on mental health and wellbeing with a wide range of communities. Using the MWIA process in Lancashire enabled us to build Social Prescribing into a range of policies, such as the Local Area Agreement and Local Strategic Partnership action plans.

In the Lancashire Local Area Agreement (LAA) we had chosen National Indicator 119 – Self-reported wellbeing – as a 'proxy' indicator for mental health. This was measured by the PLACE Survey – which asked people to rate their perception of their wellbeing and also used the abridged Warwick–Edinburgh Mental Wellbeing Scale (WEMWBS – discussed later in the chapter). NI 119 sat within the Health and wellbeing theme of the LAA but we were very conscious that mental health was a cross-cutting theme and using the MWIA allowed us to undertake a structured analysis of how action plans, programs and projects of the other several themes – economic, environment, community safety, communities, children and older people – might influence wellbeing. One of the most beneficial aspects of the process was the increase in mental wellbeing awareness among the huge range of individuals and agencies involved and the acceptance that wellbeing was 'everybody's business'.

SOCIAL PRESCRIBING IN ACTION

So what is actually prescribed and by whom? There is some controversy over the use of the word, prescribing, as it has such strong medical connotations. The North Lancashire model accepts self-referrals and referrals from non-health agencies, as well as referrals from health professionals, including GPs. Most models involve a central coordination point to which people are referred, and a form of holistic assessment of their current life circumstances.

Both Social Prescribing services in North Lancashire sit within the infrastructure of *Help Direct*. Help Direct is a service funded by Lancashire County Council and provided by a range of voluntary sector providers. The service is designed to provide people with practical support, guidance and information to get the most out of life.

The holistic assessment that is taken uses a 'life domain' format to identify social or psychological issues which impact on wellbeing, and focuses on identifying steps to address these and setting goals. Interventions are then chosen from a menu of discrete and community-based resources to support the achievement of these identified goals. Progress is evaluated against a range of outcome measures.

The life domains are:

- health and fitness,
- home and garden,
- feeling safe in your home and community,
- learning and leisure,
- managing finances,
- mobility and transport,
- community groups and involvement,
- getting the right help and support,
- relationships and families,
- employment, volunteering and training

Case Study – Angela

Angela was referred to the social prescribing service by her GP and was experiencing agoraphobia, anxiety and depression. She was spending most of her time indoors with the curtains shut. The assessment identified the impact this was having on her life. The coordinator then helped Angela define a goal to work toward.

Before she became unable to leave the house on her own, Angela was volunteering at a local school, where she listened to reading, helped with spelling and so on. Angela said that she felt useless because she couldn't even get to the school, and that when she had volunteered there, it had increased her sense of wellbeing and decreased her anxiety and depression.

Angela was given advice on managing stress and panic, and when she felt confident in managing her anxiety, she was supported to resume her volunteering. The coordinator suggested that a volunteer meet her at the door and walk

---

with her to school to enable her to do her volunteering. The volunteer would then meet her at the school at the end of the afternoon and walk back home with her.

This enabled Angela to overcome the barrier to undertaking a wellbeing-promoting activity, and the volunteering increased her sense of positivity, confidence and self-esteem and reduced her anxiety.

The holistic assessment and goal planning processes draw from motivational interviewing methodology (MI), where motivation is defined as 'a state of readiness or relatively new cognitive-behavioral technique that aims to help people identify and change health behaviors'.

The principles of MI are to help the interviewee:

- to understand his or her thought processes related to the problem;
- to identify and measure the emotional reactions to the problem;
- to identify how thoughts and feelings interact to produce the patterns in behaviour;
- to challenge his or her thought patterns and implement alternative behaviors.

Miller and Rollnick (1991) outline the eight steps of MI that allow the therapeutic process to work. These are outlined below:

1. Establishing rapport – developing a trust-based relationship between assessor and interviewee;
2. Setting the agenda – supporting the interviewee to set realistic goals;
3. Assessing readiness to change – gaining insight into the level of motivation and gently challenging that (which helps to identify potential barriers);
4. Sharpening the focus – breaking down patterns of behavior into component parts to focus on specific behaviors;

5. Identifying ambivalence – looking at reasons for existing behavior to increase insight;
6. Eliciting self-motivating statements – phrasing things in a positive way and highlighting successes;
7. Handling resistance – encouraging reflection on the change process;
8. Shifting the focus – looking at the beliefs which underlie behaviors.

Many of the Social Prescribing interventions described in this chapter will already be happening in some localities, although they may not be described in such terms. A whole system approach to Social Prescribing will build on existing arrangements and improve coordination and referral procedures. Recruiting a Social Prescribing coordinator will greatly enhance the program's success.

Central coordination can improve the efficiency and effectiveness of the service through: providing coordination of all potential referrers and referral pathways; updating the range of resources/directories of agencies and facilities to which referrers can signpost clients; identifying potential resources for assessing and addressing identified need within a supported referral framework; monitoring performance and evaluating outcomes; recruiting, training and supporting volunteer; and publicizing and raising awareness of the service.

Once an individual's needs have been identified via the holistic assessment, then he/she is encouraged to consider some realistic goals and what potential barriers may exist to achieving them. The coordinator can then, if required, suggest means of support to overcome those barriers. This could include signposting to specialist services, practical support or expert advice, opportunities for personal/skills development, methods of self-help, as well as accessing discrete sources of support available within the Social Prescribing service itself.

SOCIAL PRESCRIBING INTERVENTIONS AND THEIR EVIDENCE BASE

Financial management

Financial difficulty and debt are by far the most common stressors identified as contributing to stress and emotional distress. Debt was identified as one of the key risk factors for mental illness in the Foresight Report – even more so than low income. The suggested interventions can all be facilitated by Social Prescribing – such as financial literacy training, debt advice and benefits checks and support into employment.

Stress management skills can be delivered via a variety of formats – through self-help groups, bibliotherapy, computerized behavioral therapy and personal development or psycho-social skills training.

In North Lancashire the longest-running, and most popular and effective intervention within the Social Prescribing program is the 'Moving Forward' course.

'Moving Forward' utilizes valuable learning from Neuro-linguistic Programming (NLP), which recognizes that self-talk can be destructive, or it can be the voice of reason that changes the way things appear. The course was first developed in 2002, and over the years has developed into a model for changing destructive self-talk into a more harmonious voice.

People who attend the course come from many different backgrounds and have usually reached the proverbial 'brick wall', where directions for moving away from it are limited at best, and then often confusing. The course therefore consists of a range of subjects from everyday experiences:

- Confidence and what it means to each of us.
- Communication, both verbal and non-verbal and effective listening.

- Creativity and the resources we have that drive us.
- Goals and dreams and how to identify both.
- Assertiveness and understanding our own Bill of Rights
- Memory and its part in our self-esteem.
- Assumptions; how do we make them and what can we learn?
- Understanding change by revisiting our beliefs and values.
- Exercises that strengthen our sub-conscious mind and let it be heard.
- Fears and phobias eliminated.

Using NLP to address these and many more experiences during the course enables the participants to re-evaluate their own situation, by realizing that others have similar difficulties each day. Working together has proved very popular, and in some circumstances has produced long-standing friendships. Innate skills have come to the fore, leaving the participant in no doubt that somewhere inside, they have a wealth of assets to make changes efficiently.

The course content is never rigid, and is designed to allow choice: whether to speak out and make a point; parallel a similar situation in daily life; or agree to demonstrate an exercise for the benefit of the rest of the group. The exercises are all based on each element of the above content and have a deep impact on changing 'stuck' thinking. For example: anchors (NLP term) are prevalent in our lives whether we find them useful or not. These are situations such as tunes we may hear on the radio, which may take our thoughts immediately to a situation where we remember the tune being played, in order to re-play the event in our mind. This can be negative as well as positive, but if it is a significant event, then we have no choice at that moment but to revisit. However, by using techniques to either dispose of a memory that serves no useful purpose, so that the tune no longer has power, or enhancing the memory, if it is a reminder of something we enjoyed, and contains useful resources from the past experience, we can learn to make a choice in how we select memories and what effect these have on us. This is immediate and lasts as long as the participant wants it to. The change is so significant that others in the group are able to see visible evidence that this has worked.

At this point we can pair up and support each other with similar changes, thereby not only making a difference to our own life, but enabling someone else to find profound changes too. Being part of this epiphany is also beneficial for the value of seeing what it looks like on the outside whilst experiencing it on the inside. A holistic approach in body language and communication is important if change is to occur. And communication is a major part of the course. Understanding how we communicate and how it is received and perceived has been the most discussed subject during each of the courses delivered.

Dynamic restructuring and re-framing underpins the essence of the course but with small steps and a client-led delivery. Those that attend may start with trepidation, but many have gone on to a return to work; have been able to make the first move in long-standing disagreements; have gained more confidence to speak out and make their desires known; reduced medication or just enjoyed the experience of realising they are not alone in all this. Re-framing fear and trepidation during the weeks, into reaching for long-held goals, and breaking down any barriers placed before them, has proved that this type of course or workshop is key to encouraging each individual to Move Forward on their own terms, and at a pace that suits them. Being part of a group is vital; believing in yourself as an individual has dynamic and long-lasting results.

Alexandra L Addams, MCAHyp DABCH, NLP (master)
Website: www.nlptherapyuk.com

Another personal development course commonly referred to by Social Prescribing is the 'Feel **confident for the** future' course. This course targets people who may be feeling inadequate or having negative thoughts about themselves, and aims to help build confidence in a supportive environment and develop new interpersonal skills, thus enabling participants to become more effective in their daily life. They will look at their current situation and identify how they might start to move on by identifying some short-term goals. They will learn how to become more decisive, express their feelings openly, and feel more confident when they are communicating with others. Participants will also learn about the personal skills needed to be successful in a work context such as working with others, communication skills and organizing a workload.

Case Study

M was referred to Social Prescribing because she experiences anxiety and panic attacks and spends most of her time at home. She has no friends and her only company is her mother with whom she lives.

Following assessment it was apparent that M experienced very low levels of confidence and felt isolated. The Life Domain assessment also highlighted that M's other worry was that her house desperately needs decorating – she bought the paint two years ago, but doesn't know where to start and asked if someone could come and do it for her.

After discussion about available options, M decided that tackling her confidence and her house were her short-term goals. She decided that she would join the Feel Confident for the Future course at the Adult College. M had never previously thought of going to college – she thought that she was not clever enough, and not worthy of a place.

The coordinator arranged for a volunteer to meet with M and go to college at a quiet time to have a look a round, meet receptionists and other college staff, have coffee and just generally get a feel for it. The volunteer also arranged to meet M to accompany her to the college open day.

For her house, the coordinator suggested that it might be an idea if someone could paint with her, rather than for her, and show her how to do it.

M is very enthusiastic about both projects, and is now looking forward to starting college in September, and to learning how to paint. She says that her volunteer is great and she already feels better having been out and having something to look forward to.

LIFELONG LEARNING

'Moving Forward' and 'Feel Confident for the Future' are both examples of psycho-education and focus specifically on developing coping skills and emotional resilience. They are both delivered in partnership with local adult education services.However, any form of learning can have potential benefits for mental health – 'keep learning' being one of the *five ways to wellbeing.*

Research by the National Institute of Adult Continuing Education (NIACE) showed that opportunities for learning may impact positively on health (NIACE 2003) by improving an individual's:

- socioeconomic position
- access to health services and information
- resilience and problem-solving; and
- self-esteem and self-efficacy.

NIACE showed that adult learning is a good tool to re-motivate people with poor wellbeing or who are beginning to experience mental ill-health. This was supported by the success of pilot project to prescribe learning as part of route back into encouraging wellbeing. The project, *Prescriptions for Learning*, produced very positive results. Of the 49 people referred to a learning advisor, 46 took up their appointment and 32 went on to participate in a learning activity. When individuals were asked whether getting involved with learning had made any difference to them, the overwhelming response was 'yes' and interviewees were very enthusiastic, reporting benefits to their mental and physical health. Partnerships around health and adult education – which are a fundamental feature of most Social Prescribing models – can facilitate such benefits.

NIACE and the Inquiry into the Future for Lifelong Learning Theme Paper 4 – Wellbeing and Happiness (2007) also recognized the wider benefits of learning – not only the obvious economic benefits. The paper called for a recognition that by directing funding for learning toward types of learning that seem most likely to deliver skills, competences and employability – which seems sensible in times of financial strain – doing so ignores wider benefits.

The paper draws from the growing evidence from the science of wellbeing which suggests that people do not derive fulfillment from adequate income alone, enjoyment and fulfillment from a number of different factors. The benefits of learning impact on health and wellbeing by increasing social connections and an ability to contribute to the wider community. People gain pleasure from grappling with, mastering and then using new skills and knowledge. All in all, they value freedom and the ability to shape their own destinies.

Lifelong learning 'encourages social interaction and increases self-esteem and feelings of competency. Behaviour directed by personal goals to achieve something new has been shown to increase reported life satisfaction. While there is often a much greater policy emphasis on learning in the early years of life, psychological research suggests it is a critical aspect of day-to-day living for all age groups. Therefore policies that encourage learning, even in the elderly, will enable individuals to develop new skills, strengthen social networks, and feel more able to deal with life's challenges' (New Economics Foundation 2009).

Kolb (1993) describes learning as '*the* major process of human adaptation'. Learning occurs in all settings and at all life stages and encompasses other adaptive concepts such as creativity, problem-solving, decision making and attitude change, which all can assist in developing a sense of control, tolerance, flexibility and evaluation of alternative solutions. This will therefore have a positive influence on people's ability to build resilience to stress.

COMPUTERIZED COGNITIVE BEHAVIORAL THERAPY (CCBT)

Computers and Internet-based therapy programs have now been around for several years, and can offer an accessible and cost-effective assessment and treatment for people with mild to moderate mental distress. Within the North Lancashire Social Prescribing service CCBT is used in a variety of ways – depending on the needs and wishes of the individual client.

There are now several free-to-access CBT sites available on the Internet. CCBT is not ideal for everyone – the clients need an element of computer literacy and motivation to complete the course, but anyone who has access to the Internet can use these sites. It is a natural progression from how the Internet is used as a source of information. Powell and Clarke (2006) found that the Internet had been used as a source of mental health information by over 10 percent of the population, and by over 20 percent of those with a history of mental health problems. The majority (90 percent) of these users were 18- to 29-year-olds, both people in employment and students.

One of the difficulties in recommending CCBT within a Social Prescribing model is to ensure the effectiveness, validity and appropriateness of the site. The British Association for Behavioural and Cognitive Psychotherapies has published a useful review of these sites (Gournay 2006).

The review identified free to access websites, which we now refer clients to with confidence:

- MoodGym (http://moodgym.anu.edu.au)
- Living Life to the Full (www.livinglifetothefull.com).

The Gournay Report identifies that CCBT, including programs that are free to access, may provide users with substantial benefits – both on its own or in conjunction with other therapeutic interventions – and the benefits may increase if the user is encouraged to use the site by a professional. The report recommends that information about these websites should be made freely available.

It is also recommended that professionals working with people with emotional distress familiarize themselves with the sites and access and navigate their way through them to understand what is on offer and how it can complement other elements of a treatment plan.

In North Lancashire, explanatory leaflets about CCBT are provided in a range of settings to maximize use of the sites. The leaflets provide an overview of both the sites on offer and how to access them. It also offers an option of facilitated CCBT for those who lack the computer skills or motivation to complete the course themselves, or who would prefer the support of a group setting.

The **Living Life to the Full** course is an online life skills program developed by Dr Chris Williams, who has many years of experience using a CBT approach. This program takes users through a variety of modules with the aim of educating them around managing their problems more effectively by using CBT through the stresses and strains of life. It aims to provide access to high-quality, user-friendly training in practical approaches that people can use in their own life, using a five-area assessment model. The five areas are:

- life situations, relationships, practical resources and problems;

- altered thinking;
- altered feeling;
- altered physical symptoms;
- altered behavior.

The course content teaches key knowledge in how to tackle and respond to issues/demands which we all meet in our everyday lives, covering:

- understanding why we feel as we do;
- practical problem-solving skills;
- using *anxiety control training* relaxation;
- overcoming reduced activity;
- helpful and unhelpful behaviors;
- using medication effectively;
- noticing unhelpful thoughts;
- changing unhelpful thoughts;
- healthy living – sleep, food, diet and exercise;
- staying well.

The course is presented in an accessible way using a mix of text, audio, visual and cartoon information and is supplemented by short downloadable handouts. Moderated discussion forums are available to help course users swap ideas, information and provide mutual support.

The **Mood Gym** is a website originating in Australia. It is also an interactive web program that teaches the principles of CBT. It also demonstrates the relationship between thoughts and emotions, and works through dealing with stress and relationship break-ups, as well as teaching relaxation and meditation techniques, and again uses assessments, and a variety of media to communicate the information.

PHYSICAL ACTIVITY AND MENTAL HEALTH

The Department of Health (2001), in the National Quality Assurance Framework for Exercise Referral Systems, evidenced that physical activity reduces the risk of depression, and has positive benefits for mental health, including reducing anxiety and enhancing mood and self-esteem. Taking frequent effective exercise is one of the best physical stress-reduction techniques available. Exercise improves health and reduces stress and can also relax tense muscles and help promote sleep. Exercise has a number of other positive benefits:

- It improves blood flow to the brain, bringing additional sugars and oxygen that may be needed when thinking intensely.
- When an individual thinks hard, the neurons of their brain function more intensely. As they do this, they can build up toxic waste products that can cause foggy thinking. By exercising, the speed the flow of blood through the brain increases, moving these waste products faster.
- Exercise can cause release of chemicals called endorphins into the blood stream. These give a feeling of happiness and positively affect the overall sense of wellbeing.

Exercise also increases general physical fitness and there is also good evidence that physically fit people have less extreme physiological responses when under pressure than those who are not. This means that fit people are more able to handle the long-term effects of stress, without suffering ill health or burnout.

GPs and the wider primary healthcare team – including Social Prescribing programs – have an ideal opportunity to encourage people to increase their level of physical activity. This may be done in a variety of ways, from issuing routine advice to all patients on being more active, offering specific counseling services, recommending facilities or services such as local walking programs or referring into a specific *exercise referral system*.

In recent years, there has been a significant and sustained growth in exercise referral schemes, with the most common model being referral to facilities such as leisure centers, facilitated walks or gyms for supervised exercise programs. The aim is for these interventions to promote long-term adherence to a physically active lifestyle.

Referrals to walking programs are particularly preva lent in North Lancashire Social Prescribing – with people particularly enjoying the social element of the walk.

ARTS AND HEALTH

Other popular and effective Social Prescribing activities involve using arts and creativity. These include: arts and performance (including writing, painting, sculpture, photography, music, poetry, drama, dance and other performance arts and film); libraries; museums; heritage and cultural tourism.

'Arts on prescription' is distinct from art therapy, a professional discipline with a long tradition as a psychological therapy (Kalmanowitz and Lloyd 1997), but still has therapeutic benefits.

Evidence of effectiveness addresses three key areas:

- the impact of participation in the arts on self-esteem, self-worth and identity;
- the role of creativity in reducing symptoms (e.g. anxiety, depression and feelings of hopelessness); and
- arts and creativity as resources for promoting social inclusion and strengthening communities.

One very popular and effective intervention in North Lancashire was a Walking with Creative Minds group. This involved guided walks in the local area of natural beauty and digital photography and processing and poetry. The 'product' of the group was a presentation of poetry illustrated with imagery from the walks and shown at various festivals and events. The results for the participants was measurably increased wellbeing – it was an excellent way of putting the *five ways to wellbeing* into action through team work and socializing (connect); being active; learning new skills (photography and editing); taking notice (focusing on nature and writing poetry) and giving – all participants were involved in using the group experience in campaigns and roadshows.

BOOKS ON PRESCRIPTION/BIBLIOTHERAPY

Bibliotherapy usually takes the form of a 'prescription' or a recommendation by a GP or mental health worker for a particular book to be borrowed from a public library. Lancashire County Council Library service have been hugely supportive in implementing books on prescription across the county, and in some areas of the county bibliotherapy within a Social Prescribing model includes referral to reading groups using self-help materials.

Over half of the library authorities in England are currently operating some form of bibliotherapy (Hicks 2006). A review of research evidence for self-help interventions for people with mental health problems (Lewis and Anderson 2003) found that most studies reported a significant benefit from use of self-help materials based on CBT approaches for treatment of depression, anxiety, bulimia and binge eating disorder as a first step in a stepped-care approach. Frude (2004) found that bibliotherapy had high patient acceptability, a tendency to continued improvement over time and low relapse rates. The Lancashire scheme is based on the Cardiff model developed by Frude.

ECOTHERAPYOR 'GREEN ACTIVITY'

'Green activity' or 'ecotherapy' derive from the principles of 'biophilia' – which literally means 'love of life or living systems'. It was first used by Fromm to describe a psychological orientation of being attracted to all that is alive and vital. In such schemes participants become both physically and mentally healthier through contact with nature. This can include:

- gardening and horticulture;
- growing food;
- walking in parks or the countryside (such as the Walking with Creative Minds project);
- involvement in conservation work;
- developing community green spaces.

Green exercise (physical exercise in a natural environment) is associated with increase in self-esteem, positive mood and self-efficacy (Pretty *et al.* 2003; Countryside Recreation Network 2005).

A report commissioned from the University of Essex by MIND (MIND 2007) suggests that green activity is a cost-effective complement to existing treatment options for mild to moderate mental health problems.

VOCATIONAL SUPPORT/SUPPORTED EMPLOYMENT

Partnership work with various supported employment agencies is a feature of most Social Prescribing programs. People with mental health problems are much less likely to be employed than the population as a whole (Disability Rights Commission 2006).

The type of barriers to getting and keeping employment include:

- reduced confidence and self-esteem;
- fears about being able to cope with work;
- concerns about disclosure, employers' attitudes and explaining gaps in employment;

- concerns about finance and work;
- lack of skills, experience or qualifications and
- stigma and discrimination.

(Social Exclusion Unit 2004)

Conversely, work can also be seen as a support to wellbeing – as a source of income, positive social recognition, social integration and identity (Warr 1987). A lack of meaningful activity is one of the most common issues identified in the holistic assessment of people referred to Social Prescribing and may be a short- or long-term goal. Referrals to supported employment services, or agencies that help with job applications and interview techniques is effective for people who are work-ready. Those for whom returning to work is a longer-term goal benefit from other Social Prescribing activities focusing on developing confidence and self-esteem or may try volunteering first.

VOLUNTEERING

Volunteering has two principal roles within a Social Prescribing program – as an intervention to develop personal skills and as a valuable resource for building capacity within the program itself.

The evidence of the benefits of volunteering are well-documented and encouraging and facilitating access to volunteering activity within a Social Prescribing program may be empowering for some clients and a potential route to developing valued skills and opportunities for social contact. Casiday *et al.* (2008), in their literature review, conclude that 'volunteering was shown to decrease mortality and to improve self-rated health, mental health, life satisfaction, the ability to carry out activities of daily living without functional impairment, social support and interaction, healthy behaviors and the ability to cope with one's own illness.' Volunteering is also recommended as one of the *five ways to wellbeing* (Give).

Within the North Lancashire service, trained volunteers are an immensely valued resource, fulfilling different roles, such as:

- supporting the co ordination element of the program – assisting clients in undertaking social needs self-assessment and identifying goals;
- providing administrative support;
- supporting access to computerized CBT;
- offering intervention support as befrienders, care navigators or signposters and supporting access to other Social Prescribing interventions (co-facilitating groups; accessing education, physical activity or other classes; accessing community facilities);
- supporting clients in accessing help (such as debt counseling, housing advice, etc).

Volunteers should be employed by the service provider (usually third sector) and should have employee rights. They should be fully trained and supervised and supported in carrying out their role.

TIMEBANKS

Timebanks are the most recent addition to the North Lancashire Social Prescribing service, but the concept was developed in the mid-1980s by civil rights lawyer Dr Edgar Cahn.They are a mechanism for volunteering and at the heart of time banking is the belief in reciprocity – everyone becomes both a giver and a receiver of time. For every hour a member spends helping someone out, they will earn a time credit. Everyone's time is valued equally and one hour always equals one time credit. The time credits can then be 'spent' when the member needs something done or they can choose to donate their credits to someone else or a local community organization. Anyone can join a time bank; they are free to join and taking part does not affect an individual's tax position or entitlement to state benefits.

The core values of Timebanks are: that people are assets and everyone has something of value to contribute to their community; that actions that support communities and social capital are of immense value.

The vision of Time Banking UK is 'A world in which people may have all they need for their own wellbeing by contributing what they can to:

- Building community
- Caring for the marginalized
- Bringing up healthy children
- Fighting social injustice.'

EVALUATING SOCIAL PRESCRIBING

Two main challenges in measuring the impact of a holistic approach to wellbeing is that improvement is often subjective and the range of potential indicators is huge. Social Prescribing aims to decrease negative symptoms, increase wellbeing and address social determinants – so to evaluate the effectiveness of a referral to the service involves measuring all these things. There are a growing number of scales for measuring both positive affect and diagnosable disorder, but in North Lancashire we use the Warwick–Edinburgh Mental Wellbeing Scale (WEMWBS) and the Patient Health Questionnaire PHQ-9 for Depression. To measure progress on determinants within the life domains, we have placed a scoring system on the initial holistic assessment – this allows individuals to not only identify what factors are impacting on their wellbeing, but to subjectively score their life balance across the eight domains.

WEMWBS is a positively worded, 14-item scale with five response categories. It covers most aspects of positive mental health (positive thoughts and feelings) currently in the literature, including both hedonic and eudaimonic perspectives.

PHQ-9 offers clinicians concise, self-administered screening and diagnostic tools for mental health disorders, which have been field tested in office practice. The tool is quick and user-friendly, improving the recognition rate of depression and anxiety and facilitating diagnosis and treatment. The aim of using the latter is less about diagnosis and more about monitoring improvement in mood.

Life Domains asks people to score how they have felt about the eight different life areas over the previous two weeks – rating 1 for very unhappy up to 5 for very happy. This gives a score between 8 and 40 which indicates how people feel about all aspects of their life.

All assessment scores are recorded at the first appointment and then again when the client completes their range of interventions.

CONCLUSION

Social Prescribing supports the implementation of Positive psychology interventions – which focus on 'strengths and virtues' rather than deficits. Increasing positive emotions helps to develop cognitive and social resources – thus enhancing creativity, tolerance, generosity and productivity – which all help to build resilience in the face of adversity. This resilience can overcome long-term psychological effects of stress such as *learned helplessness*, which is a typical chronic stress situation, when a persistent feeling of total lack of control makes the avoidance of an emotionally negative situation impossible (Seligman 2000).

The dual focus of Social Prescribing is of particular value because it addresses the social and economic context of an individual's psychological skills as well as using the concept of positive psychology. It is vital to not ignore the catalysts of psychological problems such as poverty, debt and housing whilst simultaneously addressing positive psychology attributes – such as autonomy, positive affect and self-efficacy.

Social Prescribing has proven to be a very effective and valued service within a whole-systems approach to mental health within North Lancashire, and has been integrated into the overall mental healthcare pathway.

The main benefit of this integration is the increase in operational capacity in the public mental health workforce. The three paid coordinator posts are complemented by additional capacity in community activity, volunteer workforce and students on placement within the services.

Social Prescribing adds a vital layer in providing early interventions and preventing escalation of symptoms, alleviating pressures on clinical services and reducing waiting lists for treatments, so indirectly improving other services.

In supporting recovery, the project has increased throughput in Specialist Services and Support, Time and Recovery Teams who confidently discharge more patients now there are opportunities for social inclusion.

Volunteers have a range of opportunities to engage in innovative ways of supporting clients, whilst developing skills to improve work readiness and increasing their own confidence and self-esteem.

Clients have the opportunity to examine their life domains in a holistic, comprehensive way and identify priority areas to address. They are then supported with systematic goal planning and support in implementing steps to achieve these goals. The benefits have been increase in resilience, social inclusion and self-reported wellbeing (measured by WEMWBS), a reduction in negative symptomology and a reduction in requirements for psychotropic medication.

Carers of people with mental health needs are also involved in identifying goals and in developing solutions.

As a vulnerable group in their own right, they are also eligible for assessment and support through the project, and we work closely with local carer organizations.

A recently published guidance *Commissioning Mental Wellbeing* (Newbigging and Heginbotham 2010) identifies five 'best buys' for promoting community wellbeing – and proposes the implementation of a strategic and holistic approach to commissioning services and encouraging the take-up of the 'Five ways to wellbeing' – the guidance states that 'Social Prescribing can be a useful mechanism to encourage these activities especially in those who may be lonely or disconnected.'

Social Prescribing is a relatively new concept in service delivery and has become accepted and validated by referring professionals, welcomed by clients and has resulted in the growth in skills of the coordinator workforce. Users of the service have developed skills and confidence and in some cases have remained involved as volunteers and have even gone on to paid employment. The robust evaluation methods informed a business case for future sustainability of the service.

REFERENCES

Antonovsky, A. (1979) *Health, Stress and Coping* (San Francisco: Jossey-Bass Publishers).

Antonovsky, A. 1998. *The Sense of Coherence: An Historical and Future Perspective*, in H.I.E.T. McCubbin, Elizabeth, A (Ed); Thompson, Anne I (Ed);

Casiday, R., Kinsman, E., Fisher, C., and Bambra, C. (2008) 'Volunteering and Health: What Impact Does It Really Have?', Lampeter University of Wales.

Department of Health (2001) *National Quality Assurance Framework for Exercise Referral Systems* (London: DH Publications).

Department of Health (2007) *Commissioning Framework for Health and Wellbeing* (London: DH Publications).

Department of Health (2008) *High Quality Care for All: NHS Next Stage Review* (Final Report by Lord Darzi) (London: DH Publications).

Department of Health (2010) *New Horizons: Confident Communities, Brighter Futures: A Framework for Developing well-being* (London: DH Publications).

Disability Rights Commission (2006) *Disability Briefing* (Disability Rights Commission). Available online at:http://83.137.212.42/sitearchive/DRC/PDF/10_783_Disability%20Briefing%20%20March%20%202006.pdf.

Falzer, P.R. (2007) 'Developing and using social capital in public mental health', *Mental Health Review Journal*, 12 (3): 34–42.

Frasure-Smith, N. (2000) 'Social support, depression, and mortality during the first year after myocardial infarction', *Circulation*, 101: 1919–24.

Freshminds (2009) Finance: A Family Affair report, The Post office.

Friedli, L., Jackson, C., Abernethy, H., andStansfield, J. (2009) *Social Prescribing for Mental Health – A Guide to Commissioning and Delivery* (Department of Health).

Frude, N. (2004) 'Bibliotherapy as means of delivering psychological therapy', *Clinical Psychology*, 39: 8–10.

Fryers, T., Melzer, D., Jenkins, R. (2003) 'Social inequalities and the common mental disorders: a systematic review of the evidence', *Social Psychiatry and Psychiatric Epidemiology*, 38: 229–237, doi: 10.1007/s00127-003-0627-2.

Greene, J. (2000) 'Prescribing a healthy social life', *Hippocrates*, 14 (8): 1–8.

Gournay, K. (2006) *Review of Free to Access Computerised Behavioural Therapy Websites* (Bury: British Association for Behavioural and Cognitive Psychotherapies).

Harris, T., Brown, G.W. and Robinson, R. (1999) 'Befriending as an intervention for chronic depression among women in an inner city. 1: Randomised controlled trial', *British Journal of Psychiatry*, 174: 219–224.

Hicks, D. (2006) *AnAudit of Bibliotherapy/Books on Prescription Activity in England* (London: Arts Council, England).

Karlsson, H., Lehtinen,V., andJoukamaa, M. (1997) 'Psychiatric morbidity among frequent attender patients in primary care', *General Hospital Psychiatry*, 17: 19–25.

Kersnik, J., Svab, I., and Vegnut, I. M. (2001) 'Frequent attenders in general practice: quality of life, patient satisfaction, use of medical services and GP characteristics', *Scandinavian Journal of Primary Health Care*, 19: 174–177.

Kolb, D. (1993) 'The process of experiential learning', in M. Thorpe, R. Edwards, and A. Hanson (eds), *Culture and Processes of Adult Learning* (Routledge).

Lewis, G. and Anderson, E. (2003) *Self-Help Interventions for People with Mental Health Problems* (London: Department of Health).

Melzer, D., Fryers, T., Jenkins, R. (2004) *Social Inequalities and the Distribution of the Common Mental Disorders. Maudsley Monograph 44* (Hove and New York: Psychology Press).

Miller, W. R. and Rollnick, S. (1991) *Motivational Interviewing* (London: Guilford Press).

MIND (2007) *Ecotherapy: The Green Agenda for Mental Health* (London: MIND). Available online at: www.mind.org.uk/mindweek2007/report.

Moos, R. H. And Swindle R. W. (1990) 'Stressful life circumstances: concepts and measures', *Advances in Measuring Life Stress*, 6(3): pages 171–178. Article first published online: 10 FEB 2006, doi: 10.1002/smi.2460060302

NIACE (National Institute for Adult Continuing Education) (2003)*Mental Health and Social Exclusion – Social Exclusion Consultation Document: A Commentary and Response from the National Institute for Adult Continuing Education* (Nottingham: NIACE). Available online at: www.niace.org.uk.

National Institute for Health and Clinical Excellence (2004) *Depression: The Management of Depression in Primary and Secondary Care* (London: National Institute for Health and Clinical Excellence/National Collaboration Centre for Mental Health).

Newbigging, K. and Heginbotham, C. (2010) *Commissioning Mental Wellbeing for All: A Toolkit for Commissioner* (Preston: University of Central Lancashire).

New Economics Foundation (2009) *National Accounts of Wellbeing: Bringing Real Wealth onto the Balance Sheet* (London: New Economics Foundation).

Pretty, J., Griffin, M., Sellens, M. and Pretty, C. (2003) 'Green exercise: Complementary roles of nature, exercise, diet in physical and emotional wellbeing and implications for public health policy', CES Occasional Paper 2003–1, University of Essex, Chelmsford.

Social Exclusion Unit (2004) *Mental Health and Social Exclusion* (London: Office of the Deputy Prime Minister). Availableonline at: http://www.cabinetoffice.gov.uk/media/ cabinetoffice/social_exclusion_task_force/assets/publications_ 1997_to_2006/mh.pdf.

Seligman, M. E. P. and Isaacowitz, D. M. (2000) 'Learned helplessness', in E. G. Fink (ed.) *Encyclopedia of Stress*, Vol. 2 (New York: Academic Press), pp. 599–603. Warr, P. (1987) 'Job characteristics and mental health', in Warr, P. (ed.), *Psychology at Work*, 3rd edn (Harmondsworth: Penguin), pp. 247–268.

CHAPTER 7

THE ROLE OF ORGANIZATIONS IN PROMOTING HEALTH AND WELLBEING

Susan Cartwright and Cary L. Cooper

INTRODUCTION

The performance and financial health of any organization is dependent upon it having a physically and psychologically healthy workforce who are appropriately trained, well motivated and focused on their work. Interest in the concept of the 'healthy organization' has continued to grow amongst researchers, employers and policymakers throughout the developed economies as evidence mounts that absence due to psychological disorders, mainly the result of work-related stress, is growing. Implicit in the traditional concept of a healthy organization is the notion that an aggregation of individually physically and psychologically healthy workers equals a healthy company and that the foci of health promotion and wellness programs should be directed at changing the lifestyles and behaviors of the individual to reduce the risk of them becoming ill.

In 2008, two important reviews, *Mental Capital and Well Being* (Foresight 2008) and *Working for a Healthier Tomorrow* (Black 2008) were published. These reports defined a range of current and foreseeable risks to the health and wellbeing of the UK workforce. In particular, the Foresight report emphasized the role of work-related stress in contributing to the rise in mental health problems which account for over 75 percent of visits to general practitioners.

The development of mental illness is influenced by a number of psychological, biological and social factors which take the form of:

(i) Predisposing factors – factors inherent in the individual and which make the individual more vulnerable to mental illness including genes, childhood deprivation and low self-esteem.

(ii) Precipitating factors – events and/or experiences which happen to the individual and trigger or precipitate the onset of illness. These include physical injury or disease, adverse life events like redundancy or bereavement, prolonged feelings of hopelessness and inability to cope with life stresses.

(iii) Maintaining factors – factors which prolong the illness and impede recovery, such as problems with medication, lack of social support and low self-esteem. While very severe psychotic illnesses like schizophrenia have a strong genetic contribution and are rare in the working population, the non-psychotic illnesses such as depression and anxiety are not necessarily genetic and are more common. These forms of mental ill health are more likely to be caused by environmental stress emanating from events and experiences in the workplace and/or the personal domain. Therefore the workplace environment remains an important focus for stress reduction and health promotion activities.

According to Kompier (2005), much workplace stress could be reduced if organizations focused more on the work environment and the context in which work tasks are executed. Indeed, it has been argued that excessive job demands and lack of autonomy are more strongly related to health and wellbeing than person characteristics (Jeurissen and Nyklieck 2001). Job re-design and the improvement of working conditions has been central to the health strategies of many Scandinavian policymakers and organizations for many years, but has achieved less prominence in other parts of Europe. Characteristic of the Scandinavian approach has been a focus on:-

- improving working conditions
- increasing worker participation
- improving organization and job content
- flexible working and work scheduling
- increasing worker control
- increasing worker opportunities to enhance skills and personal development.

Whereas countries such as Sweden and Canada have provided financial incentives for organizations to engage in stress prevention activities, in the UK policymakers have traditionally relied upon organizational compliance with health and safety legislation as the motivator for investment in employee health. More recently, greater emphasis has been placed on arguing the business case for expenditure in employee health and wellbeing. Evidence from a review conducted by PwC based on a review of over 50 UK-based case studies found that investment in health and wellbeing programs has a positive benefit in reducing sickness absence, reduced staff turnover, reduced accidents and injuries, reduced resource allocation, increased employee satisfaction, greater productivity and a higher company profile (PwC 2008a). However, what was also clear from the review was that success was very much dependent upon designing initiatives which took account of employee needs rather than implementing 'a one size fits all' approach.

TRADITIONAL APPROACHES TO REDUCTION AND HEALTH PROMOTION

Interventions directed at tackling the problem of stress are typically regarded as operating at three levels within the stress process and categorized as being primary, secondary and tertiary.

Primary-level interventions are concerned with taking action to reduce, modify or eliminate workplace stressors (i.e. sources of stress) and so reduce their negative impact on the individual. At the same time, primary interventions also involve the creation of positive and supportive workplace cultures which recognize that stress is a feature of modern life and not necessarily a sign of incompetence or weakness. Primary level interventions need to be informed by a diagnostic stress or wellness audit and, depending upon the type of environmental stressors operating, can take a variety of forms. Such interventions might involve:

  (i) reassessing selection and training procedures to ensure that workers are competent in their jobs;

 (ii) redesigning jobs to make them more stimulating or less demanding – as people can 'rust out' as well as 'burnout' if presented with boring and repetitive tasks which do not engage their minds and/or offer little or no challenge;

(iii) increasing employee participation and communication to make people feel more valued, better informed and more able to exercise control over their work;

(iv) introducing more flexible working arrangements to help individuals maintain a better work–life balance.

Given that stress is consistently defined as a consequence of a lack of fit between the needs and resources of the individual and the demands of the job/work environment, primary-level interventions represent an attempt to adapt the environment to better fit the individual. Or, as Levi (2005) eloquently describes it, organizations need to either 'find the right shoe for the right foot' or 'adjust the shoe to better fit the foot'.

Secondary-level interventions focus on the individual and are concerned with improving and extending the physical and psychological resources of the individual to improve their resilience and to enable them to manage stress more effectively. Secondary-level interventions can also be directed at ensuring that potential health problems are promptly detected through health screening activities or providing managers with the skills to be able to identify the signs of stress in others. Examples of secondary-level interventions include stress and lifestyle education, health promotion activities, stress management training, relaxation and fitness programs as well as interpersonal skills training in areas such as time management, leadership, communication, emotional intelligence and anger management.

Investment in stress management alone as an alternative to more fundamental primary-level interventions has been commonly criticized as the 'band aid' or 'inoculation' approach. As inherent in this approach is the notion that the organization and its working environment will not change therefore the individual has to learn new ways of coping that help him or her to 'fit in' better (Cartwright and Cooper 1997).

However, to their credit, secondary-level interventions are useful in improving resilience and the ability to cope with the stressors of life more generally and not just those encountered in the workplace. For example, white-collar workers trained in meditation techniques were found to be significantly less anxious, smoked less and consumed less alcohol over a three-month period compared with a non-trained matched control group (Alexander *et al.* 1993). Furthermore, it has to be recognized that there may be times when some sources of workplace stress lie outside the control of the organization.

Tertiary-level interventions are also targeted at the individual and are directed at providing the effective treatment for and rehabilitation and recovery of those individuals who have suffered or are suffering from serious health problems.

Interventions at the tertiary level typically involve the provision of employee counseling services, absence management and return-to-work policies designed to ensure an easy transition back into the work situation after a long spell of absence. Organizations such as the emergency services and the RMG, where employees have an increased likelihood of facing violent attacks, threats and other traumatic experiences, regularly offer special debriefing counseling after critical incidents as a means of dealing with post-traumatic stress disorder. Workplace counseling has a long history. In 1915, in the United States, the first psychiatric service was introduced in Cheney Silk Company on recognition that emotionally disturbed employees were disruptive and uncooperative. It was thought that such problems could be overcome if workers were allowed to express their feelings and personal concerns. In the United States today in excess of 25 percent of the workforce and around 10 percent of the UK workforce have access to a counseling service funded by their employer.

Research evidence concerning the impact of employee counseling has been particularly positive in demonstrating that counseling reduces anxiety and depression, and improves self-esteem (Cooper and Sadri 1991; Arthur 2000, 2001). Organizations have been shown to benefit from reduced absence costs. However, counseling is unlikely to have any positive impact on improvement in work attitudes such as job satisfaction and engagement (Arthur 2001; McLeod 2001) and may even have an adverse impact (Cooper and Sadri 1991).

DEVELOPING POSITIVE WORKPLACE CULTURES

If we accept that health is more than the absence of stress and other negative states, then a truly healthy organization is one which aspires to create work environments that engender positive emotional states. Seligman and Powelski (2003), leading proponents of the 'positive psychology' movement, consider that traditional research perspectives have overwhelmingly focused on the study of negative aspects of human behavior and organizations and believe that this should be counterbalanced by the investigation of what is good and positive about individual and organizational experience. Hence, instead of asking people what is bad or wrong with their work experience researchers should adopt techniques such as appreciative enquiry and ask about what is good or right (Snyder and Lopez 2002).

Although not without its critics (Fineman 2006), positive psychology has become institutionalized into a range of educational and research programs in the United States and is considered to be a useful lens through which to engage in work–family and diversity research (Roberts 2006). In particular, the fact that positive psychology has been so enthusiastically embraced by U.S. researchers has provoked criticism on the grounds that positive self-promotion and expressed optimism are part of the U.S. 'cultural script' which is not shared by, and is less acceptable to, less individualistic cultures (Peterson 2000).

However, there is widespread agreement that people experience subjective wellbeing either through the presence of pleasant emotions such as self-evaluated happiness or when they are engaged in interesting and fulfilling activities and are satisfied with their lives. Diener *et al.* (2003) state that, from a need or goal-setting perspective, people experience subjective wellbeing when they are working toward a desirable and valued goal or end state. Such views are consistent with Ruff and Singer (1998), who summarize the core features of good health and wellbeing as leading

a life of purpose and meaning and having quality relationships with others. The experience of positive feelings has
also been shown to enhance cognitive functioning and performance by increasing information-processing speed and
the recall of information (Forgas 2001; Isen 1999). Intergenerational differences in work-related attitudes have been
shown to impact on employee needs and expectations with
job-related happiness at its lowest within the 30–40 age
range (Clark and Oswald 2002).

At a time when individuals are spending more time at
work and expected to work longer into their lives, and so
might well look to work as a means of providing meaning,
stability and a sense of community and identity in their
lives (Hoar 2004) they are often disappointed and disillu-
sioned. Compared with mainland Europe, the UK workforce
have longer working hours and spend over 60 percent of
their time at work. This means that they are more likely
to experience problems achieving a satisfactory work–life
balance and have relatively less time to recuperate and
recover from the demands of work. This may account for
the increasing problem of presenteeism in the workplace,
that is, people attending work when they are not fit to
do so. A survey of workplace absence (HSE 2005) found
that 44 percent of public sector respondents reported that
they had attended work when suffering from ill health
compared with 37 percent for the private sector. More flexible working arrangements may go some way to address
these problems. In addition, factors such as downsizing, an
increase in remote working and a greater reliance on elec-
tronic communication have only served to contribute to
heighten anxiety, emphasize discontinuity and reduce the
quality and quantity of interpersonal communication and
support (Donald 2001).

According to Herriot (2001), the resultant growth in
employee cynicism in recent years reflects the gap between
managerial rhetoric and reality present in many modern
organizations. Herriot elaborates on this by highlighting

three areas where the gaps have become obvious. First, there is the rhetoric of empowerment which emphasizes that individuals can expect more autonomy when in reality they are expected to be more compliant, to stick to the rules and be closely monitored and controlled, for example as in call center environments. Secondly, there is the managerial rhetoric of equity and justice which emphasizes fair treatment and one single and favorable employment relationship for all when in reality employees are expected to accept differences and that some individuals, for example part-time and contingent workers, may be treated less well than others. And finally, there is the rhetoric which surrounds change, as being necessary, evolutionary and rational, and emphasizes the opportunities it presents for employees to learn and increase their employability when in reality such initiatives are more likely to simply mean more work for the same rewards.

WHAT DO PEOPLE WANT FROM WORK?

In order to create a positive and healthy work environment, one needs to return to the question of what people want from work other than a means of earning a living. Money might be the primary motive that makes individuals attend work but not necessarily be a sufficient incentive to perform optimally. Back in the 1980s, Warr (1982) was one of the first researchers to pose 'the lottery question' in asking people if they would continue to work in the absence of any financial need to so. He found that over 60 percent of working-age men and women admitted that they would continue to work in such circumstances because work fulfilled a variety of needs other than financial. These needs included: activity and variety, the opportunity to learn new skills, social contact, temporal structure, a sense of achievement, status and identity and purpose (a reason to get up in the morning!). This still remains the case in that the national lottery companies continue to find that more than half of their really big winners continue to work after receiving their windfall – although not necessarily in the same jobs. When employees' needs are unmet at work, they experience disappointment, job dissatisfaction and de-motivation, which leads to physical and/or psychological withdrawal. The manifestations of physical and psychological withdrawal include absence, labor turnover, sub-optimal performance and poor health.

The work needs and values of individuals have been shown to differ and change over time largely as a result of age and career stage (Maslow 1943; Super 1957). For example, younger people may often place a greater emphasis on the social and personal development opportunities of work, those with children or other caring responsibilities might want more flexibility, and older workers might place a greater value on job security and economic stability.

The last decade has seen an increasing focus on intergenerational differences in needs, values and attitudes toward work, based on the view that shared events influence and define each generation. The Silent Generation (b. 1925–45) are regarded as having grown up in difficult times and been shaped by the experiences of harsh economic times and the adversities of war, which have served to make them a loyal, dedicated, hard-working and risk-averse workforce, grateful to have had a job. In contrast, the following generation, the Baby Boomers (b. 1946–61), grew up in optimistic and more positive times with the opportunity for social mobility and advancement through their work. Baby Boomers, more than other generations, are driven to achieve through their work and have come to be associated with workaholic behaviors because of their tendency to put work before family life often at a cost to their health and personal life. Their offspring, Generation X(b. 1962–79), commonly described as 'the latch key kids', no doubt having reflected on the lives of their working parents, are, in contrast, characterized by a greater interest in work–life balance than job status and tenure and are less respectful of authority. As Generation Y, the Internet generation (b. 1980–2000), enter the workforce, there is growing evidence that they have brought a new set of attitudes and a greater concern about ethical standards, corporate social responsibility and the wider environment and are more questioning of the status quo. Indeed, a recent survey of graduate recruitment conducted by PwC (2008b) found that 80 percent of Generation Y graduates will deliberately seek employers whose behavior in relation to corporate responsibility reflects their own values.

Whilst research on intergenerational differences has highlighted some important differences in work-related attitudes and values which employers need to take account of, it is as yet unclear whether these differences will sustain or change as the different generations work through their own life stages and adjust their expectations. However, such research has also shown some important universal needs and expectations that are common across generations. Several large-scale studies (Friedman and Greenhaus 2000; Finegold and Mohrman 2001) have shown that, regardless of age, meaningful work, skill utilization, recognition and trust, feeling valued and time for self are significant factors in predicting retention and perceptions of wellbeing.

MEANINGFUL WORK

In a study of over 10,000 young people to ascertain the characteristics of what makes 'a good job', Bibby (2001) found that respondents considered interesting work (86 percent), a feeling of accomplishment (76 percent), friendly and helpful colleagues (63 percent) and adding something to peoples' lives (59 percent) were as or more important than pay (66 percent) and job security (57 percent). It has been suggested that the essence of meaning is 'connection' and that it is this sense of connectivity that leads to performance improvement, increased commitment and employee engagement (Holbeche and Springett 2004) and wellbeing (Quick *et al.* 2002). According to Baumeister (1991), the search for meaning is driven by four individual needs which create an integrated wholeness, namely

(i) a sense of purpose;
(ii) a set of values which provide a sense of 'goodness' and positivity to life as a means for justification for action;
(iii) a sense of self-efficacy;
(iv) a sense of self-worth.

While there is no widely agreed definition of meaning in the workplace, it would seem to have two basic components – job meaning and social meaning. Job meaning involves doing an activity which is worthwhile, provides an opportunity to achieve full potential and confers a feeling of making a difference. Central to the concept of job meaning is that what one is doing is purposeful and of value. Leaders and managers can play an extremely important role as 'meaning makers' in highlighting employee contribution and value, even in relatively low-skill jobs. For example, a ward manager might highlight to hospital cleaners that their job is at the forefront of fighting disease and infection and not just a set of routine and menial tasks. Social meaning derives from having quality relationships with work colleagues, a good work–life balance and a feeling of belonging. The promotion of social interaction as a means of creating a sense of belonging and meaning has often been neglected by organizations as constituting a distraction from the serious business of work. Yet, a survey of the top 50 rated employers in the UK, which included the highly profitable Microsoft (*Sunday Times* 2001) found that 91 percent of employees described their company as a friendly and fun place to work which went to great lengths to provide opportunities for interaction and socializing amongst its employees.

Seligman and Powelski (2003) differentiate between living a pleasant life, a good life and a meaningful life. They regard a pleasant life which is reflected in sensual pleasures(e.g. material life) as the lowest form of happiness, closely followed by a good life, associated with enjoying something we are good at, and a meaningful life, doing something one believes in, as providing the highest level of attainment and most lasting form of happiness. Such ideas date back to Aristotle and the notion of eudemonia, a form of happiness achieved by living virtuously and attaining goals that have intrinsic value.

QUALITY RELATIONSHIPS

Many years ago, Kahn and colleagues (Kahn *et al.* 1964) demonstrated that poor working relations and mistrust of work colleagues can lead to psychological strain. Since then, many studies (Cooper *et al.* 2001) have shown that supportive and considerate managers directly enhance health and help individuals to cope with work pressures. A survey of HR professionals and managers conducted in the UK found that 95 percent of those surveyed rated supportive managers as the workplace factor most likely to help employees cope with stress (Industrial Society 2001) and that one out of three employees cite their line manager as the key reason for wanting to leave an organization. Therefore, it is not surprising that the behaviors of line managers and others in leadership roles have a significant impact on the psychological wellbeing of individuals and the work team who report to them (Robertson and Flint-Taylor 2008).

Prospective medical studies conducted over the last 30 years have consistently shown that those who are most socially isolated and 'disconnected' are at increased risk of ischemic heart disease, whereas the presence of helpful and positive social relationships have been found to promote general wellbeing and are protective against physical harm. However, it is has been shown that only one in four UK workers reported having close work relationships and only 18 percent of individuals work for organizations that provide opportunities to develop friendship with work colleagues.

FIVE WAYS TO WELLBEING

The recent Foresight report (2008) outlined five simple ways of achieving happiness – *connect, be active, be curious, learn* and *give* – which reinforce the notion what it means to lead a meaningful life. Although very much directed at the individual, these signposts to happiness have the potential to be adapted by organizations and incorporated into their health and wellbeing strategy.

Connect

The connect message emphasizes the importance of developing relationships with family, friends, colleagues and neighbors as a means of enriching one's life and gaining support. There are many ways in which the individual can enact this message, for example sitting down to share a family meal – at a table and without a television on – or offering to mow an elderly neighbor's lawn.

Organizations can encourage the development of relationships between work colleagues in a number of ways, including providing social spaces in which employees can meet and relax, encouraging employees to take regular breaks, ensuring that team meetings provide the opportunity for members to exchange views and ideas rather than simply a means of passing on information as well as celebrating successes and achievements and injecting some fun into work. By introducing work–life balance policies and ensuring that individuals do not work excessive hours, employers can also help employees to remain better connected with their family and friends.

Be Active

The *be active* message encourages individuals to become more engaged in sports and hobbies and other forms of physical activity. Individuals can increase their mobility and fitness simply by walking more, for example using the stairs rather than the elevator, using their cars less or taking their dog (or their neighbor's dog) for a walk.

As demonstrated by earlier evidence (Chapter 3), there is much that organizations can do to encourage increased physical activity through fitness advice, the provision of subsidized gym membership and the distribution of pedometers so that employees can monitor their activity levels. Managers could also encourage team walks or try to identify other activities where there is a collective interest in doing something together, maybe investing in a Wii-Fit games console for the staffroom.

Be Curious

The advice from the Foresight report (Cooper *et al.* 2009) is that individuals need to be more attentive to the beauty of everyday moments as well as the unusual on the basis that reflecting on these experiences helps the individual to appreciate what matters to them. This is probably one of the hardest messages to stimulate but might involve encouraging people to stop and pause to take photographs to capture these positive experiences, record experiences in diaries or take time out to visit areas of natural beauty, art galleries and places of historical interest.

Training in relaxation, yoga and mindfulness techniques have been shown to be a trigger for stimulating curiosity and appreciation and such activities could form the basis of a useful organizational intervention. There is also much that organizations can do in the design and decoration of work spaces that can improve employee mood and open them to new experiences through art displays, wall paintings and so on.

Learn

Learning new skill and acquiring new knowledge, for example learning to play an instrument or learning a foreign language, has been long recognized as a means of providing challenge and satisfaction as well as providing fun and improving confidence. Organizations can stimulate learning through the investment of both work-related and non-work-related learning resources and/or letting people have an hour of two off work to spend on learning activities. Organizations such as Mersey Travel have a scheme to promote informal learning by providing interest-free loans to fund personal learning activities, which is paid back directly through salaries. Fletchers Bakeries in Sheffield introduced a 'Six Book Challenge' as part of their Learning at Work Day to encourage workers to read six specific titles. They have since arranged for a mobile library to visit the bakery once a month and introduced a Book Swap Club. Such activities have significantly contributed to improve the literacy levels of their factory workers.

Give

The *give* message emphasizes that helping friends and strangers is very rewarding and links individual happiness to a wider community. There is plenty of evidence (Black 2008) that volunteering is beneficial to health and wellbeing and has become an integral part of social prescribing (Chapter 6). Voluntary work can be undertaken as a corporate as well as an individual level activity. Employers such as Provident Financial and Co-Operative Financial Services have encouraged their employees to undertake extensive programs of voluntary work to improve local neighborhoods and schools and many companies encourage team participation in charity fundraising events. For workers who may find it difficult to accept that the job they do is of itself meaningful, the opportunity to engage in external activities supported by their organizations, such as volunteering, can give them the sense that they are able to make a difference.

CONCLUSION

The concept and meaning of employee health has widened considerably in recent years to encompass not only the prevailing conditions and factors that can potentially make people fall ill but also the aspects of work and life that positively enhance health and promote wellbeing. This more holistic approach has switched the responsibility for employee health and wellbeing as exclusively the concern of occupational health doctors and professionals to it becoming a much wider organizational remit and a key organizational performance indicator.

The opportunities to be innovative in the field of health and wellbeing are immense and exciting. It is hoped that this book has provided some new ideas and experiences which will serve to further stimulate this field.

REFERENCES

Alexander, C. N., Swanson, G. C., Rainforth, M. V., Carlisle, T. W., Todd, C. C. and Oates, J. R. (1993) 'Effects of the transcendental meditation program on stress reduction, health and employee development: a prospective study in two occupational settings', *Anxiety, Stress and Coping*, 6: 245–262.

Arthur, A. (2000) 'Employee assistance programmes: the emperor's new clothes of stress management', *British Journal of Guidance and Counselling*, 28 (4): 549–559.

Arthur, A. (2001) 'Mental health problems and British workers: a survey of mental health problems in employees receiving counselling from employee assistance programmes', *Stress and Health*, 18 (2): 69–75.

Baumeister, R. F. (1991) *Meanings of Life* (New York: Guildford).

Bibby, R. W. (2001) *Canada's Teens: Today, Yesterday and Tomorrow* (Toronto, ON: Stoddart).

Black, C. (2008) *Working for a Healthier Tomorrow* (London: Department of Work and Pensions).

Cartwright, S. and Cooper, C. L. (1997) *Managing Workplace Stress* (Thousand Oaks CA: Sage).

Clark, A. E. and Oswald, A. J. (2002) 'A simple statistical method of measuring how life events affect happiness', *International Journal of Epidemiology*, 31 (6) 1139–1144.

Cooper, C. L. and Sadri, G. (1991) 'The impact of stress counselling at work', in P.L. Perrewe (ed.), *Handbook of Job Stress* (Special Issue), *Journal of Social Behaviour and Personality*, 6 (7): 411–423.

Cooper, C. L., Dewe, P. J. and O'Driscoll, M. P. (2001) *Organizational Stress: A Review and Critique of Theory, Research and Applications* (Thousand Oaks, CA: Sage).

Cooper, C. L., Field, J., Goswani, U., Jenkins, R. and Shakian, B. (2009) *Mental Capital and Well Being* (Oxford: Wiley Blackwell).

Diener, E., Lucas, R. E. and Oishi, S. (2003) 'Personality, culture and subjective well-being: emotional and cognitive evaluations of life', *Annual Review of Psychology*, 54: 403–426.

Donald, I. (2001) 'Emotion and offices at work', in R. L. Payne and C. L. Cooper (eds), *Emotions at Work* (Chichester: Wiley), pp. 281–306.

Finegold, D. L. and Mohrman, S. (2001) *What Do Employees Really Want ? The Perception vs the Reality* (New York: Korn Ferry International).

Fineman, S. (2006) 'On being positive: concerns and counterpoints', *Academy of Management Review*, 31 (2): 270–292.

Foresight (2008) *Mental Capital and Well Being* (London: Government Office for Science).

Forgas, J. P. (2001) *Feeling and Thinking: The Role of Affect in Social Cognition* (Cambridge: Cambridge University Press).

Friedman, S. D. and Greenhaus, J. H. (2000) 'Work and family–allies or enemies?' *Psychology of Women Quarterly*, 25 (3): 259–279.

Health and Safety Executive (HSE 2005) *Survey of Workplace Absence Sickness and (ill) Health* (London: HSE).

Herriot, P. (2001) 'Future work and its emotional implications', in R. L. Payne and C. L. Cooper (eds), *Emotions at Work: Theory, Research and Applications for Management* (Chichester: Wiley).

Hoar, R. (2004) ' Work with meaning', *Management Today*, May: 44–50.

Holbeche, L. And Springett, N. (2004) *In Search of Meaning in the Workplace* (UK: Roffey Park Institute).

Industrial Society (2001) *Improving Skills in the UK Workforce* (London: Industrial Society).

Isen, A.M. (1999) *On the Relationship between Affect and Creative Problem Solving* (London: Taylor and Francis).

Jeurissen, T. and Nyklieck, I. (2001) 'Testing the vitamin model of job stress in Dutch healthcare workers', *Work and Stress*, 15 (3): 254–264.

Kahn, R. L., Wolfe, D. M., Quinn, R. P., Snoek, J. D. and Rosenthal, R. A. (1964) *Organizational Stress: Studies in Role Conflict and Ambiguity* (New York: John Wiley).

Kompier, M.A. (2005) 'Dealing with workplace stress', in C. L. Cooper (ed.) *Handbook of Stress, Medicine and Health* (London: CRC Press).

Levi, L. (2005) 'Spice of life or kiss of death', in C. L. Cooper (ed.), *Handbook of Work and Health Psychology* (London: CRC Press).

Maslow, A. (1943) 'A theory of human motivation', *Psychological Review*, 50 (4): 370–396.

McLeod, J. (2001) *Counselling in the Workplace* (London: British Association for Counselling and Psychotherapy).

Peterson, C. (2000) 'The future of optimism', *American Psychologist*, 55: 44–55.

PwC 2008 (a) *Building the Case for Wellness* (London: PwC). Available online at: www.workingforhealth.gov.uk.

PwC 2008 (b) *Graduate Survey: Millennial Expectations and Attitudes* (London: PwC).

Quick, J. C., Cooper, C. L. Quick, J. D. and Gavin, J. H. (2002) *The Financial Times Guide to Executive Health* (London: FT/Prentice Hall).

Roberts, L. M. (2006) 'Shifting the lens on organizational life: the added value of positive scholarship', *Academy of Management Review*, 31 (2): 292–306.

Robertson, I. T. and Flint-Taylor, J. (2008) 'Leadership, psychological well being and organizational outcomes', in S. Cartwright and C. L. Cooper (eds),*The Oxford Handbook of Organizational Well Being* (Oxford: Oxford University Press).

Ruff, C. D. and Singer, B. (1998) 'The contours of positive human health', *Psychological Inquiry*, 9 (1): 1–28.

Seligman, M. E. P. and Powelski, J. O. (2003) 'Positive psychology: FAQs', *Psychological Inquiry*, 14: 159–169.

Snyder, C. R. and Lopez, S. J. (2002) *Handbook of Positive Psychology* (Oxford: Oxford University Press).

Super, D. E. (1957) *The Psychology of Careers* (New York: Wiley).

Warr, P. B. (1982) 'A national study of non-financial employment commitment', *Journal of Occupational Psychology*, 51 (2): 183–196.

INDEX